Volume **14 THE**
GOLDEN BOOK
ENCYCLOPEDIA

Pacific Islands to population

pa-pop

An exciting, up-to-date encyclopedia
in 20 fact-filled, entertaining volumes

Especially designed as
a first encyclopedia for
today's grade-school children

More than 2,500 full-color
photographs and illustrations

GOLDEN ®

From the Publishers of Golden® Books

Western Publishing Company, Inc.
Racine, Wisconsin 53404

ILLUSTRATION CREDITS
(t=top, b=bottom, c=center, l=left, r=right)

1 l, John Rice/Joseph, Mindlin & Mulvey, Inc.; 1 r, David Rickman/Publishers' Graphics; 3 b, Jack Fields/Photo Researchers; 4 b and 5, David Lindroth Inc.; 6 br, David Lindroth Inc.; 7, Joel S. Fishman/Photo Researchers; 8 tr, Scala/Art Resource; 9 both, Superstock; 10 tl, Giraudon/Art Resource; 10 tr, © ARS N.Y./SPADEM, 1988/Art Resource; 11 tl, Greg Heins/Art Resource; 11 tr, Porterfield/Chickering/Photo Researchers; 12 bl, Marion H. Levy/Photo Researchers; 12 cl, David Lindroth Inc.; 13, Jack Fields/Photo Researchers; 14 tl, Kenneth W. Fink/Bruce Coleman Inc.; 14 cl, National Zoological Park, Smithsonian Institution; 14 cr, Michael Collins/Stock, Boston; 15 t, Tom Powers/Joseph, Mindlin & Mulvey Inc.; 16 tl, Didier Givois/Agence Vandystadt/Photo Researchers; 17 tl, Jeff Foott/Bruce Coleman Inc.; 17 b, © Joe Viesti; 18, Joseph Nettis/Photo Researchers; 19, Martin Helfer/Shostal Associates; 19 br, Bettmann Archive; 20-21 b, Peace Corps; 21 tr, Renee Purse/Photo Researchers; 22 tl, Lloyd P. Birmingham; 23, Historical Pictures Service, Chicago; 24 tl, Bettmann Archive; 24 br, David Rickman/Publishers' Graphics; 25, John Rice/Joseph, Mindlin & Mulvey, Inc.; 26, Laura Riley/Bruce Coleman Inc.; 27, NASA; 28 tr, Marilyn Bass; 29 bl, Peter Guttman/Bruce Coleman Inc; 30 cl and 31-32 all, John Rice/Joseph, Mindlin & Mulvey Inc.; 34, Turi MacCombie/Evelyne Johnson Associates; 35 b, Giraudon/Art Resource; 36 bl, Victor Englebert/Photo Researchers; 37 tr, reprinted from *Peter Pan*, copyright 1987 by dilithium Press, Ltd., and used by permission of Crown Publishers; 38, E.R. Degginger/Bruce Coleman Inc.; 39 t, Walter Gaffney- Kessell/Publishers' Graphics; 39 inset, Geoffrey Gilbert/Photo Researchers; 40, Richard Hutchings; 41 both, Arthur Sirdofsky; 42 t, Joseph Nettis/Photo Researchers; 42 inset, Bettmann Archive; 43 bl, © Joe Viesti; 44-45 b, Michael O'Reilly/Joseph, Mindlin & Mulvey; 46, Richard Hutchings; 47, Photograph by Edward Weston/© 1981 Arizona Board of Regents/Center for Creative Photography; 48, Richard Quataert/Taurus Photos; 49 all, Susan Goldstein; 50 tr, James Bell/Photo Researchers; 50 b, Lloyd P. Birmingham; 51 tr, Phil Degginger/Bruce Coleman Inc.; 51 b, Turi MacCombie/Evelyne Johnson Associates; 52-53 t and 53 tr, Tom Powers/Joseph, Mindlin & Mulvey Inc.; 54, Courtesy of Yamaha Music Corp., USA, Piano Division, Buena Park, California; 55 tr, © ARS N.Y./SPADEM, 1988/© Museés Nationaux France; 55 br, Raph Gatti/Sygma; 56 tr, L.L.T. Rhodes/Taurus Photos; 58, Walter Gaffney-Kessell/Publishers' Graphics; 59, Juan Barberis/Melissa Turk & The Artist Network; 60-61 t, Historical Pictures Service, Chicago; 61 br, Kent and Donna Dannen/Photo Researchers; 62, Hans Reinhard/Bruce Coleman Inc.; 63 tl, Bettmann Archive; 63 br, Historical Pictures Service, Chicago; 64-65, Victor Englebert/Photo Researchers; 66, Tom Powers/Joseph, Mindlin & Mulvey Inc.; 68, David Parker/Science Photo Library/Photo Researchers; 69 and 70, Turi MacCombie/Evelyne Johnson Associates; 71 tl, H.A. Thornhill, APSA, ARPS/National Audubon Society/Photo Researchers; 71 br, Nuridsany et Pérennou/Photo Researchers; 72 tr, Turi MacCombie/Evelyne Johnson Associates; 72 bl, Farrell Grehan/Photo Researchers; 73, Tanya Rebelo/ Joseph, Mindlin & Mulvey Inc; 74 bl, Juan Barberis/Melissa Turk & The Artist Network; 75, Craig Hammell/The Stock Market; 76, American Petroleum Institute; 77, Terry Eiler/Stock, Boston; 78, Douglass Baglin/National Audubon Society/Photo Researchers; 79 bl, Philip Greenberg/ Photo Researchers; 79 br, Martha Swope; 80, Blair Seitz/Photo Researchers; 81, Martha Swope; 82, David Lindroth Inc.; 83 t, Eunice Harris/Photo Researchers; 85, Lloyd P. Birmingham; 86 tr, OKAPIA/Photo Researchers; 87, Susan Kuklin/Photo Researchers; 88, Leonard Freed/Magnum; 89 tl, Joe Traver/Gamma-Liaison; 89 tr, Diego Goldberg/Sygma; 91, © ARS N.Y./Pollock-Krasner Foundation, 1988/Art Resource; 92, David Lindroth Inc.; 93 t, © Joe Viesti; 93 br, Scala/Art Resource; 94 tl, David Lindroth Inc.; 94 br, Historical Pictures Service, Chicago; 95, G. Giansanti/Sygma; 96, Walter Gaffney-Kessell/Publishers' Graphics.
"The Red Wheelbarrow" on page 83 is from William Carlos Williams, *Collected Poems, Volume I: 1909-1939*, copyright 1938 by New Directions Publishing Corporation. "The Panther" on page 84 is from Ogden Nash, *Verses from 1929 On*, copyright 1940 by Ogden Nash. The poem first appeared in *The Saturday Evening Post*, and is reprinted by permission of Little, Brown and Company.

COVER CREDITS
Center: Farrell Grehan/Photo Researchers. Clockwise from top: Geoffrey Gilbert/Photo Researchers; Bettmann Archive; National Zoological Park, Smithsonian Institution; Laura Riley/Bruce Coleman Inc.; Nuridsany et Pérennou/Photo Researchers; Tom Powers/Joseph, Mindlin & Mulvey Inc.

Library of Congress Catalog Card Number: 87-82741
ISBN: 0-307-70114-X

ABCDEFGHIJK

The letter *P* began as the ancient Egyptian word picture that stood for "mouth."

 The Semites used this symbol for their letter *pe*, which was their word for "mouth."

The Greeks called this letter *pi*. Their symbol for it looked like a hook.

P

Pacific Islands

The world's largest ocean, the Pacific, has more islands than any other ocean. There may be as many as 30,000 islands scattered over an area about the size of North America. Many are little more than patches of sand, some without names. Yet New Guinea, the largest Pacific island, is the second-largest island in the world—after Greenland.

The Pacific Islands formed in different ways. Wake Island is an *atoll*—a round island built up of coral skeletons. Like other atolls, Wake Island has a *lagoon*—a shallow body of water—at its center. The Northern Marianas, Fiji, and Vanuatu are the tops of volcanoes. Islands in the Pacific can form and disappear very quickly. Volcanoes are still active, and fierce storms can wash away the smaller islands. (*See* **island**.)

The Pacific Islands—also called *Oceania*—are divided into three groups—Polynesia, Melanesia, and Micronesia.

Polynesia means "many islands." It is the largest island group and stretches about 5,000 miles (8,000 kilometers) from north to south. Hawaii, Western and American Samoa, and Tahiti are Polynesian Islands.

West of Polynesia is Melanesia. The name means "black islands." The group got its name because the people living on these islands have dark skin. Melanesia includes New Guinea, Fiji, the Solomon Islands, and New Caledonia.

The ocean provides people who live on the Pacific Islands with food and a way to get around. The outrigger on this man's canoe gives it balance in the waves.

PACIFIC ISLAND COUNTRIES AND TERRITORIES

Name	Status	Capital	Square Miles	Square Kilometers	Population
American Samoa	U.S. territory	Pago Pago	76	197	34,000
Cook Islands	New Zealand assoc.	(none)	91	236	20,000
Easter Islands	Chilean territory	(none)	63	163	2,000
Fiji	independent	Suva	7,055	18,272	700,000
French Polynesia	French territory	Papeete on Tahiti	10,210	26,444	175,000
Guam	U.S. territory	Agana	212	549	123,000
Kiribati	independent	Bairiki, on Tarawa	278	720	51,000
Marshall Islands, Republic of the	independent	Majuro	69	179	39,060
Micronesia, Federated States of	independent	Kolonia, on Ponape	41	106	6,448
Midway Islands	U.S. territory	(none)	2	5	2,220
Nauru	independent	Yaren	8	21	8,000
New Caledonia	French territory	Noumea	7,358	19,057	150,000
New Zealand	independent	Wellington	103,736	268,676	3,271,000
Niue Island	New Zealand assoc.	(none)	100	259	5,000
Northern Mariana Is.	U.S. territory	(none)	183	474	21,065
Palau, Republic of	independent	Koror	178	461	13,772
Papua-New Guinea	independent	Port Moresby	178,259	461,691	3,326,000
Pitcairn Is. Group	British territory	(none)	7	18	65
Solomon Islands	independent	Honiara	10,983	28,446	273,000
Tokelau	New Zealand terr.	(none)	4	10	2,000
Tonga	independent	Nuku'alofa	270	699	103,000
Tuvalu	independent	Fongafale, on Funafuti	10	26	7,000
Vanuatu	independent	Vila, on Efate	5,700	14,763	132,000
Wake Island	U.S. territory	(none)	3	8	1,647
Wallis & Futuna Is.	French territory	Mata-Utu	106	275	9,000
Western Samoa	independent	Apia	1,097	2,841	163,000
TOTAL			326,099	844,596	8,638,277

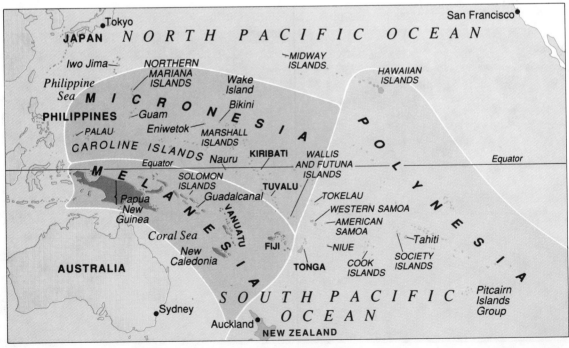

North of Melanesia is the island group of Micronesia. Micronesia—meaning "small islands"—includes the Marshall Islands, Palau, and the Federated States of Micronesia.

About 11 million people live on the Pacific Islands. Hundreds of languages are spoken there. Most Islanders are Christians, but they often follow their traditional religions, too. For many Pacific Islanders, life is not much different than it was for their ancestors. Most people live in small fishing or farming villages. They grow their own fruits and vegetables and catch fish, crabs, lobsters, and turtles from the ocean. Men and women wear loose cotton dresses, grass skirts, or bands of cloth. Their homes are built from grass and trees. But air travel, tourism, and military bases on the islands have introduced changes, even on the smaller islands. New Zealand and Hawaii have large cities and the most modern ways of life. (*See* **Hawaii** and **New Zealand**.)

Traditional ways began to change in the 1500s, when European ships started crossing the Pacific Ocean. France, Spain, Portugal, and England claimed many of the islands as their own. Today, many of the Pacific Islands are again independent nations. The Republic of the Marshall Islands, the Republic of Palau, and the Federated States of Micronesia are the newest.

Pacific Mountain System

The Pacific Mountain System is made up of several mountain ranges along the Pacific coast of North America. Most of the ranges run in a north-south direction. They include many offshore islands that are actually the tops of underwater mountains.

The Pacific Mountain System has beautiful scenery. There are forests, valleys, rivers, lakes, snowcapped peaks, and *glaciers*— giant rivers of ice. A wide variety of plants and animals live there. Large sections of the system are set aside as parks.

The Coast Mountains form the largest section of the system. These mountains hug the western coast of Canada and include Vancouver Island.

The Alaska Range forms the northern part of the system. Mount McKinley is in the Alaska Range. At 20,320 feet (6,194 meters) tall, it is the highest mountain in North America. (*See* **McKinley, Mount.**)

The Saint Elias Mountains, in Alaska and Canada, have peaks that are more than 17,000 feet (5,182 meters) above sea level. Mount Logan is 19,850 feet (6,050 meters) tall. It is the highest point in Canada and the second-highest in North America.

The Cascade Mountains extend from Canada through Washington, Oregon, and California. There are many volcanoes in the Cascades. One of them, Mount St. Helens, erupted in 1980. (*See* **St. Helens, Mount.**)

The Sierra Nevada is the mountain range along the California-Nevada border. It contains stands of towering sequoia trees. Sequoias are among the oldest and largest

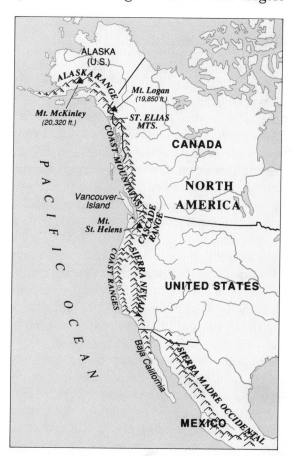

living things on earth. The redwood, a kind of sequoia, can reach heights of 300 feet (91 meters).

A great deal of rain falls in the northern ranges. Dams across many of the rushing rivers provide water for irrigation and hydroelectric power.

The water and hydroelectric power are needed in the southern part of the system, called the Coast Ranges. There the mountains are lower and receive much less rain. They are rich in gold and petroleum. Millions of people live in the Coast Ranges. The two largest cities are Los Angeles and San Francisco, in California. (*See* **Los Angeles** and **San Francisco**.)

The Pacific Mountain System is separated from the Great Plains of the United States and Canada by the Rocky Mountains. In the southwestern United States, the Great Basin wedges between the Sierra Nevada and the Rockies.

Pacific Ocean

The Pacific is the world's largest ocean. It covers about one-third of the earth's surface. It washes the shores of Asia and Australia on the west, and of North America and South America on the east. It extends from Antarctica in the south to the Arctic Ocean in the north. From east to west, the Pacific Ocean is about 11,000 miles (17,600 kilometers) wide—about four times the distance across the continental United States. From north to south, it measures about 9,000 miles (14,400 kilometers). In all, from the warm tropics to the frigid poles, the Pacific covers 64 million square miles (166 million square kilometers). All of the continents and islands of the world could fit into the area covered by the Pacific—with plenty of room to spare.

Smaller bodies of water, called seas and gulfs, branch off the Pacific. The Sea of Japan, China Sea, Sea of Okhotsk, Yellow Sea, and Gulf of California are among the largest.

The Pacific is also the world's deepest ocean. It has an average depth of 14,000 feet,

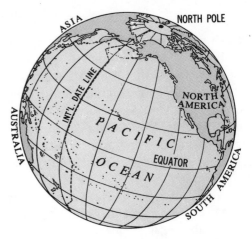

or about 2½ miles (4.2 kilometers). The ocean floor is cut by deep trenches—between 20,000 and 30,000 feet (6 and 9 kilometers). In the northern part of the ocean, trenches follow the line of the Aleutian Islands and Kamchatka. There are also deep trenches in the southwestern part of the ocean. The deepest of all is the Mariana Trench, off the island of Guam. It is 36,198 feet (10.9 kilometers) deep—almost 7 miles.

Beneath the waters of the Pacific are high ridges and deep *trenches*—valleys.

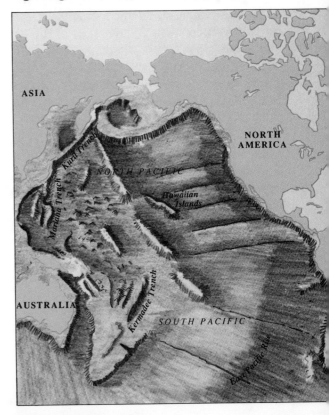

There are about 30,000 islands scattered over the vast Pacific. Many of these islands are mountains and volcanoes that rise above the water. The East Pacific Ridge runs along the ocean floor from Antarctica to North America, near Mexico. It is part of the Mid-Ocean Ridge—a ridge system that runs through all the world's oceans.

A series of volcanoes, called the Ring of Fire, circles the main ocean basin. Scientists estimate that half the islands of the Pacific were formed by volcanic activity. Volcanic eruptions have also destroyed entire islands.

Underwater earthquakes in the Pacific cause huge ocean swells called *tsunamis* (soo-NAH-meez). A tsunami can be 100 feet (30 meters) high and can travel at 400 miles (640 kilometers) per hour. Sometimes these giant waves are called "tidal waves," even though they are not caused by tides.

In 1513, Vasco Núñez de Balboa, a Spanish explorer, walked west across the Isthmus of Panama and saw a huge unexplored ocean. Ferdinand Magellan was the first European to sail across this ocean. He named it the Pacific, which means "peaceful." In his journal, Magellan wrote of calm seas and gentle breezes. (*See* **Balboa, Vasco Núñez de** and **Magellan, Ferdinand.**)

But storms over the Pacific can be extremely violent. *Typhoons* are the most severe storms. They are tropical cyclones or *hurricanes*—storms that move in a giant circular pattern. A typhoon's winds often exceed 150 miles (240 kilometers) per hour. The storms bring heavy rains and cause widespread damage. But they also bring needed fresh water to the Pacific islands. Every year, about 120 typhoons form in the Pacific. They usually strike during a period of three to four months.

The tropical zones near the equator can be the stormiest parts of the ocean. Yet at certain times of year, the wind completely dies down in the tropical zones, which sailors called the *doldrums*. The lack of wind in the doldrums sometimes stalled sailing ships for weeks or months. North and south of the doldrums, sailors could count on steady winds, called *trade winds*. Sailing ships carrying goods for trade relied on these winds to hurry them from North America to Asia.

The Pacific is also the world's largest habitat for marine life. The ocean is home to thousands of kinds of monerans, protists, plants, and animals. The rocks, cliffs, and sand beaches of the shores are homes for birds and other animals that spend part of their lives in the ocean. (*See* **ocean plants.**)

Scientists believe there may be forms of life yet to be discovered in the Pacific. They also think there are great mineral riches, including oil and metals, on or beneath the ocean floor.

The Pacific is so vast and deep that it has not yet been completely explored. People cannot even send submarines to the deepest parts of the ocean, because the pressure of the water would crush them. Scientists can only guess at what kind of life may exist in the deepest waters.

The Pacific Ocean is the world's largest ocean. Its name means "peaceful."

paint

We use paints to protect and decorate surfaces. The glossy paint on a steel car body protects it against rust. Paint on wooden outdoor furniture protects it from rain and sun. Paint adds color to our surroundings. For thousands of years, people have used paint to create art. (*See* **painters and painting.**)

Paint is a liquid that contains *pigments* —very small particles that give the paint its color. Even white paint is colored with pigments. Paint also contains a *binder,* which acts like a glue. When the paint dries, the binder forms a smooth coat. To make the paint thin enough to spread, a *thinner* is added. The paint may also contain a *drier* to help the paint dry quickly.

The binder in some paints is an oil, such as linseed oil. An oil-based paint will not wash off with water. Many paints used to paint rooms or houses use *latex* as a binder. Latex contains small particles of rubber or plastic. While latex-based paints are still wet, they can be washed off with water. Once they dry, the small particles stick together, and the paint cannot be washed away. Latex paints are thinned with water, and oil-based paints are thinned with turpentine or paint thinner. Although latex-based paints are easier to use and clean up after, oil-based paints protect better and last longer.

Every year, people in the United States use about 6,064 million liters (1,600 million gallons) of paints. Latex paints account for one-fourth of the total amount.

Paints are brushed, rolled, or sprayed onto a surface. Some work best on paper or wood. Other paints are made for cement, metal, plastic, and glass.

Early peoples found pigments in nature—for example, in berries, plant roots, and clay. They mixed them with water or animal fat. The oldest paints we know of were used to paint pictures inside caves about 50,000 years ago. This is an amazing length of time for paint to last.

PAINTERS SEE THE WORLD IN DIFFERENT WAYS

A man goes to market in this simple scene painted in a book during the Middle Ages.

painters and painting

Painting is the act of applying colors and lines to create a picture. People who do this are known as painters. They use skill and imagination to create works of art.

Almost everyone has made a painting at some time in his or her life. People who are talented and who study painting may become painters. Some of them create paintings that people buy. Many people also enjoy painting as a hobby.

Painters use a wide variety of tools and materials. Three things they must have— paint, something to paint on, and something to paint with.

Paint Paint is made of *pigments* mixed in a *medium.* Pigments are small particles of the substances that give the paint its colors. Pigments may be chemicals or ground-up minerals, or metals such as gold or lead.

A dance scene painted in the 1500s (left) is filled with life and movement. In the 1700s dance scene (right), the large, airy room is more important than the dancers.

The medium may be glue, egg yolks, or certain vegetable gums and vegetable oils. Paints that use glues or vegetable gums are called *watercolors*. The medium in *tempera* is egg yolk. *Oil paints* use vegetable oils as their medium. A paint's medium and pigments give it a certain look. Each kind of paint is used in a different way.

Surfaces for Painting A painter paints on a surface called a *support*—it supports the paint. Oil painting is usually done on a linen or cotton canvas support stretched on a frame. Tempera often has a wooden panel as a support. Watercolor is usually applied to paper. Painters have also used cardboard, particle board, and even walls.

Before they can be painted on, canvas and wood are usually coated with a *ground*—a substance that keeps the paint from soaking into the support. The ground on canvas may be white paint or *gesso*—a mixture of plaster and water. Wood takes gesso as a ground. Once the ground is dry, the painter may begin painting.

After an oil or tempera painting is finished and thoroughly dry, it is coated with a thin layer of varnish. Varnish protects the painting from light, dust, and pollutants.

Applying the Paint Painters usually apply paint with brushes. Brushes come in a range of sizes. The bristles are generally animal hair. Today, many artists' brushes have artificial bristles. Brushes with soft bristles are best for watercolors and tempera. Stiffer bristles work well with oil paint.

Painters sometimes use a *palette knife*—a small, flexible spatula. The palette knife is used for mixing oil paints, applying paint, and scraping paint off the canvas.

Before beginning a painting, many artists draw the picture on paper, or sketch the picture lightly on the wood, canvas, or paper.

In the 1890s, Cezanne used deep colors and a simple design to show a woman at home (left). Picasso's 1937 painting of a woman (right) is a collection of flat shapes.

Making drawings and sketches lets the painter try out different *compositions*—different ways of arranging the parts of the design. Some artists prefer to plan their picture as they paint and do not make a sketch before beginning.

If the painter plans to use oil paint, a *palette* is prepared. A palette is a flat, usually oval, wooden plate. The palette may also be a sheet of glass or plastic, or a tablet of waxed paper. Painters arrange the oil paints on the palette according to color, so they know just where to look for them. The first row of colors includes white, yellows, reds, greens, browns, and black. The next row has blues. The last row contains *tints*—colors mixed with white. Flesh tones and sky are two of the things tints are used for.

Tempera and watercolor paints tend to be more watery than oil paints. They are mixed in dishes that have small wells.

Becoming a Painter A painter has to learn how to prepare a support, mix colors, use different paints, draw, and paint with various brushes. Art classes given by schools and art museums teach these skills.

To learn more about painting, many artists study the subject in school. They study the work of the great painters of the past. At the same time, they practice by creating their own paintings.

Some people train to become painters by working as an assistant to a painter. An assistant, called an *apprentice,* learns by painting details in large paintings, mixing colors, drawing sketches, and watching the "master" painter work. In return, a master painter tells the apprentice what is being done and why. The master will also suggest ways of improving an apprentice's own paintings.

A room where a painter works is called a

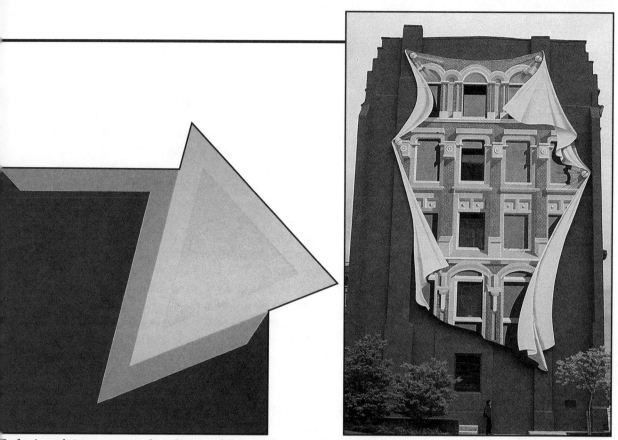

Today's painters want to break out of flat surfaces and regular shapes.
At left, a painting on a shaped canvas. At right, a huge painting seems to be part of a building!

studio. In addition to space for supplies and paintings, a studio should have plenty of light. Often, studios have windows in the ceiling, called *skylights.* Most painters prefer to have windows that face north, so the studio gets even light all day. Many painters paint outdoors, too.

Each painter has his or her own way of seeing things and of painting. These different ways of looking at and representing things are called *styles.* Part of becoming a painter is developing a style. Some painters use one style for several years before trying another.

Some painters create paintings using just lines, shapes, and colors. These painters try to show how something feels and moves, instead of what it looks like. Paintings like this are called *abstract.*

Where Paintings Are Displayed Painting is a way of communicating thoughts and feelings. So a finished painting needs to be shown. Most professional painters display their paintings in art galleries, where anyone who wants to can come and look. Art collectors visit the galleries and sometimes buy paintings.

Art museums buy paintings, too. Sometimes, they buy newly made paintings. But most often art museums buy paintings from art collectors. Also, collectors sometimes decide to *donate*—give—paintings to museums. (*See* **art museum.**)

Most painters think that having a museum display a painter's work is a great honor. It means that the paintings will be seen for many, many years.

See also **Degas, Edgar; Homer, Winslow; Leonardo da Vinci; Michelangelo; Moses, Grandma; O'Keeffe, Georgia; Picasso, Pablo; Pollock, Jackson; Rembrandt van Rijn; Renoir, Pierre-Auguste;** and **Wyeth, Andrew.**

Pakistan

Capital: Islamabad
Area: 310,403 square miles (803,944 square kilometers)
Population (1985): about 99,199,000
Official language: Urdu

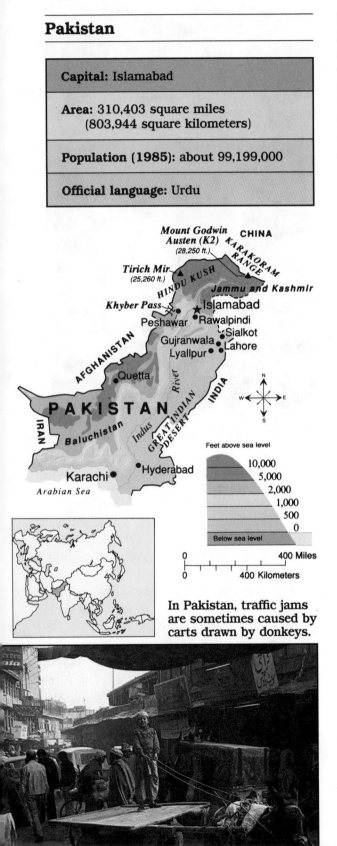

In Pakistan, traffic jams are sometimes caused by carts drawn by donkeys.

Pakistan is a nation in south-central Asia. Its southern edge faces the Arabian Sea, an arm of the Indian Ocean. It shares borders with Iran, Afghanistan, China, and India. Until 1947, Pakistan was part of India.

The northernmost part of Pakistan is in the Himalayas, the world's highest mountains. Along the eastern border with India, the land is flat and dry. Part of the Thar Desert is in this region.

The Punjab Plain and the Sind Plain cover the central region. Although they receive little rain, irrigation makes them productive farmland. The Indus River and its *tributaries*—rivers that flow into a large river—bring plenty of water.

One of the world's oldest and greatest civilizations grew along the Indus River about 4,500 years ago. This civilization—called the Indus Valley civilization—lasted about 700 years.

In the year 711, Arab invaders brought the Islamic religion to the region. For centuries, the area was ruled by Muslims—followers of Islam. Then, in the 1700s, the Muslim rulers became weak, and the area came under British control. By 1858, Pakistan was part of the British colony of India. Muslims were a minority in India, and felt they were treated unfairly. In the early 1900s, they began to demand their own separate state.

When India became independent from Britain, in 1947, a separate Muslim state was created—Pakistan. It was made up of two parts. West Pakistan consisted of the land that is today's Pakistan. East Pakistan was more than 1,000 miles to the east. In 1971, it became the country of Bangladesh. (*See* **Bangladesh**.)

Pakistan is very crowded. Its land area is slightly larger than the state of Texas, but it has more than ten times as many people. Most Pakistanis are very poor. They make their living as farmers or herders. Only about one of every four Pakistanis lives in a city. One major city is Islamabad, the capital. The largest city is Karachi, a port city on the Arabian Sea.

Pakistan's government is trying to improve the nation's economy. The major industry today is the manufacture of cotton textiles. Pakistan also has oil refineries and produces leather goods, chemicals, cement, steel, silk, wool, and sugar. Fishing is important along the Arabian Sea.

palm tree

Palms are plants native to tropical regions. Few palms have branches, and none has the woody trunk we think of trees as having. The trunk of a palm tree is actually more like a stalk. A crown of large leaves grows from the top of the palm tree's trunk. Palm trees look very different from lilies and grasses, but they are related to them.

Palm trees grow in warm places all over the world. In the United States, they grow mainly in Florida, California, and Hawaii. They may also be found in *oases*—desert areas that have underground water.

A boy shinnies up the trunk of a coconut palm tree to pick a coconut.

In Asia, there is a palm that looks like a vine. Its leaves hook onto a tall tree. As it grows, it uses its leaves to climb the tree. In South America, there is another vining palm. Other palm plants are more like shrubs and grow a cluster of stems.

Palm trees give us dates, coconuts, and other useful products. In some tropical areas, the coconut palm has many important uses. The fruit is filled with a sweet liquid called *coconut milk*. The flesh of the coconut can be eaten raw or added to cooked food. It also contains an oil used to make margarine, shampoo, soap, skin creams, and makeup. Fibers from the coconut husk are used to make rope. The trunk of the coconut palm is used like wood, and the leaves are used for roofs.

Panama, *see* Central America

Panama Canal, *see* canal

panda

There are two kinds of panda—the *giant panda* and the *lesser panda.* The two kinds do not look alike. But they behave in much the same way.

The giant panda is a kind of bear. It has black ears, black legs, and a black band over its back. A patch of black circles each eye. The rest of the panda's body, including its small tail, is white. Giant pandas may weigh more than 100 kilograms (220 pounds). They are clumsy on the ground, but they are excellent climbers. When they sense danger, they quickly go up a tree, often carrying their babies with them. At first, the babies are very tiny. At birth, they weigh about 100 grams (3 ounces), and are blind and almost hairless. A mother panda usually holds her baby close to her chest to protect it and keep it warm. The baby grows quickly. When it is about 45 days old, its eyes open. At 75 days, it begins walking.

The red panda, above, looks like a raccoon. The giant panda, left, loves to eat bamboo. Both kinds live in China.

Giant pandas are rare. They live only in certain forests in China and eat chiefly bamboo. The Chinese consider the pandas a national treasure, and have set aside special areas for them.

The lesser panda is also known as the "red panda." It is in the raccoon family and is about 91 centimeters (3 feet) long, including its long, bushy, ringed tail. It has a red coat, with white around the ears, eyes, nose, and mouth. The lesser panda lives in mountain forests in China and Nepal.

pantomime

Pantomime is a way of acting out stories without speaking. Also called *mime,* this form of acting has been used since ancient times. Actors who do pantomime are called *mimes, pantomimes,* or *pantomimists.*

Mimes use their entire bodies to act out stories. A mime uses facial expressions and body movements to show emotions and to show the kind of person being played. One mime can act the parts of different kinds of people just by sitting, standing, and walking in different ways.

A talented mime can make the audience "see" invisible things. When a mime pretends to be climbing a mountain or walking against a strong wind, you can almost see the mountain and feel the wind. A mime can even seem to change into an object. For example, a mime may start the act as a seed, grow into a plant, and bloom as a flower.

Circus clowns often perform in pantomime. Many silent-movie actors—such as Charlie Chaplin and Buster Keaton—were skillful mimes.

Mimes use movement and facial expressions to tell a story and to express feelings.

Marcel Marceau, a French mime, has helped keep mime popular. He has performed all over the world and started a school that teaches the art of mime.

See also **actors and acting** and **movie.**

paper

Paper is made from dried, pressed plant fibers. Chemicals and pigments are often added to change its color and brightness.

Paper is used to write and print on. It is made into packages, bags, wrappers, tissues, towels, and even clothes and money. But we have not always had paper.

HOW PAPER IS MADE

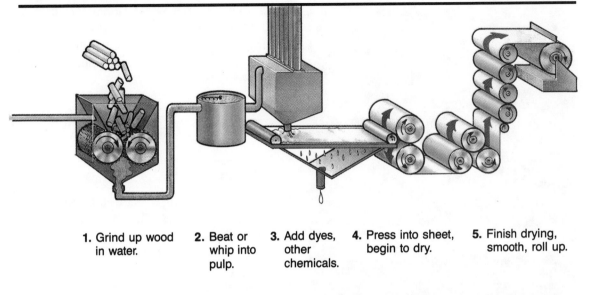

1. Grind up wood in water.

2. Beat or whip into pulp.

3. Add dyes, other chemicals.

4. Press into sheet, begin to dry.

5. Finish drying, smooth, roll up.

About 6,000 years ago, the Egyptians began making a thin, flat writing surface from the papyrus plant. They cut the stems of the plant into long strips, laid the strips across each other, and pressed out the water. The plant's juice glued the strips together into sheets. The Greeks and Romans wrote on *parchment*—treated animal skins.

About 2,000 years ago, the Chinese began making paper. They pounded the inner bark of the mulberry tree until its fibers separated. They mixed the fibers with water to make a pulp. They then dipped a screen into the pulp, lifted the screen, and let the water drain. The sheet of wet pulp left on the screen was removed and pressed. When it dried, it was a sheet of paper held together by the crisscrossed fibers and the plant gums. The Chinese also used cotton and a plant called *hemp* to make paper.

In Europe and the Middle East, people continued to write on parchment. The knowledge of papermaking reached the Middle East about 1,200 years ago, and Europe about 800 years ago. In Europe, paper was made from linen and cotton rags.

Paper, and the invention of movable type in the 1400s, helped make books less costly.

Parchment took a long time to make, and papyrus plants grew only in Egypt. This made both of them expensive. Paper was cheaper, because it could be made quickly from many kinds of plant fibers. Unlike parchment, it was easier to print on and did not damage the type. (*See* **printing**.)

In the middle 1800s, inventors found ways to make paper from wood. Wasps also use wood fiber to make their paper nests. Paper made from wood pulp eventually turns yellow and brittle. The best papers are made from plant fibers such as linen, cotton, and mulberry. Such papers can last hundreds of years.

Today's papermaking machines can produce a roll of paper that is 9 meters (30 feet) wide and 750 meters (2,500 feet) long in only one minute. The world uses about 90 billion kilograms (200 billion pounds) of paper every year. About 27 billion kilograms (60 billion pounds) of the paper goes into newsprint, books, writing, copying, and computer printouts.

Papua New Guinea, *see* Pacific Islands

A sky diver floats above the countryside in his parachute.

parachute

A parachute is like a giant umbrella. It is usually used to slow down a fall. It works by catching the air, just as an umbrella sometimes catches the wind. Unlike an umbrella, a parachute has an opening in the middle to let some air pass through. This helps keep the parachute from being pulled out of control by gusts of wind. Parachutes used to be made of silk. Today, they are made of nylon.

The first successful parachute jump was made in France in 1783—more than a century before the Wright brothers invented the airplane. The parachutist, Louis-Sébastien Lenormand, jumped from an upper-story window of a house. In 1797, people began to parachute from balloons.

Harry A. Doucett, a navy machinist, invented a better parachute. It was used to make the first successful jump from an airplane, in 1912. After that, *paratroopers*—soldiers wearing parachutes—were moved into battle from airplanes.

Today, we use parachutes to drop packages of food, medicine, and other emergency supplies to people in hard-to-reach areas.

Parachutes are also used to bring spacecraft back to earth, to slow jet planes for landing, and even to help high-speed cars stop. Skydiving—jumping with a parachute from an airplane—has become a very popular sport. (*See* **diving**.)

Paraguay, *see* South America

parasite

A parasite is a living thing that lives in or on another living thing. The thing on which a parasite lives is called its *host*. Parasites depend on their hosts for food.

Many parasites cannot be seen without a microscope. Some microscopic roundworms are parasites. They often live in the intestines of animals and take much of their hosts' food. This may make the hosts very weak. Some bacteria and protozoans are parasites. They can cause diseases, such as malaria. Humans and other animals are affected by them. (*See* **ameba** and **malaria**.)

Some parasites are large and easy to see. Tapeworms are large parasites that live in the intestines of many animals, including humans. A tapeworm is very thin, so food passes easily from its host into its body. The tapeworm's head has hooks that attach to the lining of its host's intestines. The rest of the tapeworm is made up of flat square sections, one after another. Each section is filled with eggs. A tapeworm may grow to be 6 meters (20 feet) long.

Leeches are related to earthworms, but they are parasites. They attach to an animal's skin and suck its blood. Leeches are most common in swampy areas in warm parts of the world.

Fleas are smaller than shown here. They make dogs and cats itchy.

Fleas are parasitic insects. They live on the skin of many warm-blooded animals, including dogs, cats, and squirrels. They bite the

This dodder plant is a parasite. It gets its food from the plant it lives on.

Some plants are parasites. Mistletoe is a green parasitic plant that grows on old, dying trees. It can make some of its food but must get the rest from its host. Dodder is a yellow or orange parasitic vine. It gets all of its food from the host plant.

Many parasites live with their hosts for a long time. Usually they do not kill their hosts, they only make them weak. It is better for the parasite if the host lives. When the host dies, the parasite loses its food and its home. The parasite must find a new home to survive.

animal to get its blood. Ticks are parasites that are related to spiders. A tick buries its head into the skin of warm-blooded animals and takes their blood. The tick's body swells as it fills with blood. (*See* **tick**.)

Certain fungi are parasites. Ringworm and athlete's foot are skin diseases caused by parasitic fungi. Like other fungi, the ones that cause these diseases like warm, damp places to live. Damp feet and scalps make good homes for them. (*See* **fungus**.)

Paris

Paris is the capital and largest city of France. Known as the "city of light," it is one of the world's most beautiful and important cities. For centuries, Paris has been a center of the arts, learning, and fashion. It is also famous for its wonderful foods and wines.

Paris is in northern France, about 110 miles (176 kilometers) southeast of the English Channel, in a region of rich farmland. The Seine River runs through the center of Paris, from east to west. In the middle of the

Paris has attracted artists, poets, and students from all over the world. Visitors can ride to the top of the Eiffel Tower (left) and look out on the "city of light."

Seine, and at the very center of the city, is an island called the *Île de la Cité*—"Island of the City." This is the site of the original settlement of Paris. The Cathedral of Notre Dame is on the island. The cathedral was started in 1163 and took more than 100 years to complete. It is one of the city's most famous landmarks.

The Seine River divides Paris in two. North of the river is the "right bank," the center of business, industry, and government. To the south is the "left bank," the center of arts and learning.

Paris is famous for its wide, tree-lined boulevards. The best known of these is the Champs-Élysées. At one end is a huge stone monument, the Arc de Triomphe—"Arch of Triumph." It was built by the French emperor Napoleon I in the early 1800s. He wanted a monument to his great military victories. (*See* **Napoleon.**)

At the other end of the Champs-Élysées is a square named the Place de la Concorde—"Place of Peace." It has not always been peaceful in Paris. Between 1789 and 1799, during the French Revolution, the

Older parts of Paris have many narrow, winding streets.

French king and queen and hundreds of other people were beheaded at the Place de la Concorde. (*See* **French Revolution.**)

Perhaps the most famous landmark in Paris is the Eiffel Tower. This 984-foot (300-meter) steel tower was built in 1889 for the Paris Exposition, a large international fair. At that time, it was the tallest structure in the world.

Another landmark is the Louvre, a great art museum that contains many of the world's most famous works of art. Beginning in the 1500s, Paris was a center of painting and sculpture. Many of the world's great artists lived and worked in Paris.

A tribe called the Parisii lived on the Île de la Cité in ancient times. In 52 B.C., the Romans set up a colony on the island. The colony grew, and became known as Paris around the year 300. The area that is now France was known as Gaul until 511. By that time, a Germanic tribe called the Franks had seized control of the region and made Paris their capital. France is named for the Franks.

Paris grew into a city in the late 1100s and 1200s. During these years, the townspeople built the huge cathedral of Notre Dame. Later, during the 1500s, French kings wanted to make Paris the world's most beautiful city. They planned the wide boulevards and built many grand palaces and stately buildings that are still standing today. (*See* **Louis XIV.**)

Parts of Paris were burned during the French Revolution. But within a few years, the city was rebuilt. Artists and writers came to Paris once again to learn and work.

Today, Paris is a city of more than 2 million people. Another 6 million live in smaller cities and towns nearby. Millions of visitors come to the city every year to visit its museums and landmarks. Yet Paris is also an important manufacturing and trading city. Its huge factories produce cars and other industrial goods. Its best-known products are high-fashion clothes, perfumes, and jewelry, for which it is famous worldwide.

Passover is celebrated with a *seder*—a meal of special foods.

Passover

Passover is a Jewish holiday. It celebrates the *Exodus*—the escape of the Jewish people from slavery in Egypt thousands of years ago. As the story is told in the Bible, God punished Egypt with ten plagues because the Egyptian pharoah refused to allow the Israelites—the Jews—to leave Egypt. Jewish homes were "passed over" when the tenth plague came upon Egypt. The word *Passover* also refers to the passing of the Jews from slavery to freedom when the pharoah finally let them go. (*See* **Bible** and **Israelites**.)

Passover begins on the evening before the 15th day of the Jewish month of Nisan. That is in March or April. The main celebration takes place at home on the first night, with a meal called a *seder.* Orthodox Jews have a second seder the following night. At the seder, people eat foods that have special meanings. For example, unleavened bread called *matzo* is eaten. Unleavened bread is flat, because it has nothing in it to make it rise. Matzo reminds Jews that their ancestors left Egypt in such a hurry that they could not wait for their bread to rise. Other seder foods—such as hard-boiled eggs and bitter herbs—have special meanings, too.

At the seder, Jews read the story of Exodus aloud from a book called the *Haggadah,* to remind themselves of God's help during the Exodus.

In Israel and among some Reform Jews, Passover is celebrated for seven days. Most other Jews celebrate for eight days.

See also **Judaism**.

Pasteur, Louis

Louis Pasteur was a French scientist who lived from 1822 to 1895. He found that diseases are caused by *microbes*—germs. Microbes are tiny living things. They can be seen only with a microscope.

Pasteur started working with microbes when a winemaker asked him why some wine was spoiling. Wine is made by adding yeast to grape juice. At that time, people thought yeast was a chemical that turned grape juice into wine. Pasteur guessed correctly that yeast was a microbe that changed sugar to alcohol. He thought the wine was spoiling because other kinds of microbes were getting into the grape juice. (*See* **yeast**.)

Louis Pasteur learned to vaccinate animals and humans against several diseases.

Pasteur did a lot of experiments to test his idea. He showed that different microbes change sugar into different products, such as alcohol and acetic acid. He suggested that diseases were caused by microbes.

People thought then that live microbes could come from nonliving things. Pasteur proved this idea to be wrong. He showed that microbes come only from other, parent microbes. He proved that foods could be protected by destroying the microbes already present and then sealing the food to keep others from getting in. He introduced a method of heating foods to kill harmful microbes. This method, called *pasteurization,* is widely used to kill germs in milk.

Pasteur thought that diseases could be kept from spreading if people followed better habits of cleanliness. He also developed *vaccination*—a way to prevent disease that was discovered by Edward Jenner. A person or animal is infected on purpose with weak microbes of a disease. The body develops antibodies to fight that disease. If exposed to it again, the person or animal will be *immune* —will not get sick. (*See* **Jenner, Edward.**)

Pasteur vaccinated some birds with cholera microbes. Later, when they were exposed to the disease, they did not get sick. He also vaccinated sheep and goats against a disease called anthrax. Pasteur also showed that rabies was caused by a germ so small that it could not be seen even with a microscope. He produced a rabies vaccine for dogs, and successfully treated people who had been bitten by rabid dogs. (*See* **vaccine.**)

Pasteur became famous all over the world. He died in 1895.

See also **disease and sickness.**

Paul

Paul was a missionary. He spread the new Christian religion to the cities around the Mediterranean Sea. His story is told in the New Testament of the Bible. (*See* **Bible.**)

Paul was born in the city of Tarsus (now part of Turkey) about five years after the birth of Jesus. His parents named him Saul, and he grew up believing strongly in Jewish teachings. As a young man, he went to the city of Jerusalem to study Judaism. There he met Jews who had become followers of Jesus. Saul felt this was wrong. He had the new Christians arrested and punished.

One day, Saul was riding his horse to the city of Damascus. Suddenly, he was surrounded by a bright light. He was thrown from his horse. A voice spoke to him. It was the voice of Jesus. Saul's whole life was changed by this experience. He took a new name, Paul, and began preaching about Jesus to the people of the Mediterranean world.

As he traveled, Paul kept in touch with new Christian believers by writing them letters. These letters, called *epistles,* are part of the New Testament. Christians still read and study them today.

See also **Jesus** and **Christianity.**

Peace Corps

The Peace Corps is an organization of the U.S. government. The Peace Corps sends Americans to poor countries to help the people there improve their living conditions.

Peace Corps members also hope to promote world peace and friendship.

Peace Corps members live among the people of the country in which they serve. They do many jobs, such as teaching school and caring for the sick. They also help people raise better crops, build roads, and run small factories.

Peace Corps members are volunteers who serve for two-year terms. To join, a person must be a U.S. citizen and at least 18 years old. Volunteers receive several weeks of training and are paid living expenses while they are overseas. When they return home at the end of their service, they are paid a small salary.

The Peace Corps was started by President John F. Kennedy in 1961. Since then, over 120,000 Americans have served in Africa, Asia, Latin America, and the Pacific Islands. One of the best-known Peace Corps volunteers was Lillian Carter, whose son, Jimmy Carter, became the 39th president of the United States. She volunteered when she was 67 years old, and served in India. Today there are about 5,000 Peace Corps volunteers working in over 60 countries.

A Peace Corps volunteer teaches people on a Pacific Island about good nutrition.

A peacock hopes to impress a peahen with his beautiful tail feathers.

peacock

The peacock—the male *peafowl*—is one of the handsomest of all birds. He has a train of long, colorful feathers attached to his tail. To attract females, he lifts the train and spreads the feathers like an open fan. This display may last for less than a minute or longer than an hour. During this time, the peacock does a dance, turning slightly from side to side on his heavy legs. The females—called *peahens*—are a dull grayish color and do not have trains.

There are three kinds of peafowl, all belonging to the pheasant family. Green peafowl and blue peafowl are natives of Asia. The males of both these kinds have *eyespots* on their train feathers. Eyespots are large green or blue spots that look like shiny eyes. Green and blue peacocks may weigh as much as 5 kilograms (11 pounds). Their trains may be 1.5 meters (5 feet) in length. A smaller kind is the Congo peafowl, which lives in Africa. The male is colorful, but he does not have eyespots on his train.

Even the largest peafowl can fly. In parks and zoos, you may spot them roosting in high trees. Peacocks nest on the ground. They eat grains and grasses, insects, and even snails and frogs.

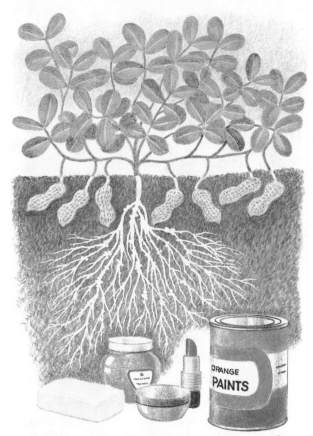
Peanuts grow underground. They are used for food and other products.

peanut

A peanut is not really a nut. It is the fruit of the peanut plant, a member of the legume family. Some peanut plants look like small bushes. Others grow along the ground. Both kinds of plants have yellow flowers. The flowers put out long stalks, called *pegs,* that reach downward and push into the ground. A shell with the peanuts inside develops at the end of the peg. Because peanuts grow undergound, they are also called *groundnuts* or *earthnuts.* Another name, *goobers,* comes from Africa.

Peanuts are an important food. They are a rich source of vegetable oil and protein. They may be ground into peanut butter or eaten whole. They may be raw, roasted, or cooked in vegetable stews and meat dishes.

Besides being food, peanuts have many other uses. Peanut oil is used not only for cooking, but to make soaps, cosmetics, paints, machine oils, and explosives. The solid part of the peanut left after the oil is removed is fed to farm animals. Powdered peanut shells are added to plastics and wallboard.

Peanuts were first grown in South America. Today, most peanuts are grown in Africa and Asia. China and India are the world's major growers of peanuts. In the United States, large crops grow in Georgia, Alabama, and North Carolina.

pearl

Pearls are gems made by mollusks with shells, especially oysters and mussels. The most valuable pearls are made by a kind of oyster that lives in tropical seas. The mussels that produce pearls live in rivers and lakes.

Pearls are usually white, but some are colored. The most valued ones are perfectly round. Pearls are used for jewelry and to decorate precious objects.

Mollusks with shells have a fold of tissue called the *mantle* around a soft body. The mantle produces the materials that form the hard shell—including its pearly inner lining, called *nacre* or *mother of pearl.* Sometimes a grain of sand or another tiny object gets

Pearls form from material that lines the inside of a mollusk's shell.

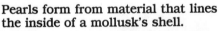

pearl forming

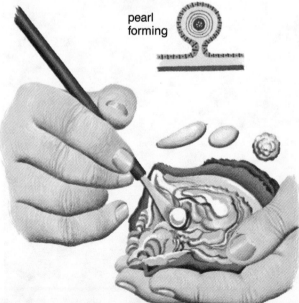

Japan's surprise attack on Pearl Harbor, on December 7, 1941, destroyed ships and planes and killed thousands. The next day, the United States entered World War II.

between the shell and the mantle. The mantle coats the object with the same pearly material, layer by layer. When the object is large enough, it separates from the shell's inner layer. It is now a true pearl.

People make *cultured pearls* by putting tiny bits of sand or other materials inside mussels or oysters and then returning the animals to the water. After a year or longer, the animals are removed from the water and opened. Only a very few of them will have produced a beautiful round pearl.

See also **gem; clams and mussels;** and **oyster.**

Pearl Harbor

Pearl Harbor is a natural harbor of Oahu Island in Hawaii. It has been a major United States naval base since 1900. It is best known, however, because the Japanese bombed it on December 7, 1941. This surprise attack brought the United States into World War II.

The attack came at 7:55 on a Sunday morning. Japanese airplanes carrying bombs and torpedoes swooped down on the U.S. fleet. U.S. soldiers, sailors, and airmen awoke with alarm and raced to their guns.

They were too late. Within two hours, enormous damage had been done. At least 18 ships were sunk or badly damaged. About 190 U.S. planes were destroyed and another 160 were badly damaged. Over 2,300 American servicemen and women were killed, and many more were wounded. Many civilians, too, were killed or wounded.

The next day, President Franklin D. Roosevelt asked Congress to declare the United States at war with Japan. Congress agreed, and on December 8, 1941, the United States entered World War II. "Remember Pearl Harbor" became a rallying cry for Americans during the war.

See also World War II.

Peary, Robert E.

Robert Edwin Peary was an American explorer of the Arctic. In 1909, he led the first expedition that reached the North Pole.

Peary was born in Cresson, Pennsylvania, in 1856, but soon moved with his family to Maine. There, he later attended Bowdoin College and graduated in 1877 with a degree in engineering. He spent several years in the U.S. Navy, then set out to become the first man "who stands at the top of the world."

The American Robert Peary and his party were the first men to reach the North Pole.

Peary's first two attempts to reach the Pole, in 1898 and 1905, were unsuccessful. During the first expedition, Peary suffered from frostbite and lost eight toes.

In 1908, Peary tried again. With 24 men, he set out from his camp at Ellesmere Island, 450 miles (720 kilometers) from the Pole. The men battled the wind and cold. According to plan, a few men at a time turned back at each stage of the trip, after helping the expedition forward. Only four Eskimo and Peary's assistant, Matthew Henson, were still with Peary on April 6, 1909, when he reached the North Pole. He planted the U.S. flag there and then started the long journey back to camp.

Peary was made an admiral and received many other honors when he returned to the United States. He died in 1920.

peas, *see* beans and peas

Pecos Bill

Pecos Bill is a character in American legend, invented by Edward O'Reilly in an article published in 1923. Later, other people made up more tall tales about this giant cowboy's adventures and skills.

One story tells how he lassoed and rode a tornado to win a bet. As he crossed the country, the storm rained out from under him and carved out the Grand Canyon.

Other stories say Pecos Bill dug out the Rio Grande with his hands and taught broncos to buck. He also tamed a mountain lion, which he rode instead of a horse.

According to legend, when Pecos Bill was a baby in the 1830s, he fell out of his family's covered wagon and into the Pecos River. They did not notice he was gone until it was too late to go back. Luckily, a pack of coyotes took a liking to the little boy and adopted him. Bill grew up thinking he was a coyote. One day, a cowboy saw him and told him he was a boy. The cowboy convinced Bill by pointing out that he had no tail. After this, Pecos Bill decided he would be a cowboy. Soon he was the best.

Some people say Pecos Bill died from laughing too hard. But others say he is still riding his mountain lion around the American Southwest.

See also **tall tale** and **myths and legends.**

Storytellers say that Pecos Bill still rides his mountain lion in the Southwest.

Peking, *see* **Beijing**

pelican

The pelican is a large water bird with a long, hooked bill. A big pouch of skin hangs from the bill. The pelican uses its pouch to scoop up and store fish. Later, it swallows some of the fish and feeds the rest to its young. The pouch has another function. On hot days, a pelican cools off by opening its mouth and letting water evaporate from the inner wall of the pouch.

There are six kinds of pelicans, two of which live in North America. The largest is the *American white pelican.* It may be 1.8 meters (6 feet) long and have a wingspan of more than 2.7 meters (9 feet). It lives along lakes, swamps, and seacoasts.

The second North American pelican is the *brown pelican.* It is the smallest pelican, reaching lengths of just over 1.2 meters (4 feet). The brown pelican lives along sea-coasts. It is the only pelican that dives. From 8 or 9 meters (26 to 30 feet) above the water, it watches for schools of fish. When it spots a school, it dives headfirst with a loud splash. Moments later, it comes up with a fish in its pouch.

Other pelicans feed by dipping their bills into the water as they fly along. Sometimes, a group of pelicans fish together. When they spot a school of fish, they form a line between the fish and the open water. Then they slowly fly toward shore, beating the water with their wings. This drives the fish into shallow water. The pelicans close a circle around the fish and then scoop them up.

On land, pelicans waddle. But in the air, they are very graceful. They are strong fliers, and may travel long distances in search of food or when they migrate. Sometimes a group of pelicans flies in a perfect formation—a straight line or a V shape. They even beat their wings all at the same time.

Pelicans nest in large groups called *colonies.* They build their nests in trees or on the

A pelican spears fish with its bill.
It carries food in a pouch under its bill.

ground. The parents take turns sitting on the eggs. They care for the babies until the young pelicans are ready to be on their own.

penguin

The penguin is a bird that walks upright and cannot fly. It has white feathers down its front and black ones covering its head, back, and wings. Many penguins can only hop or waddle on land, but they are excellent swimmers and divers. Their wings are shaped into powerful flippers that help them swim underwater at speeds up to 25 kilometers (15 miles) per hour. This speed helps penguins escape from killer whales, seals, and other enemies.

Penguins spend most of their lives in the water. They eat fish, squid, and shrimp. They come on land to mate, lay eggs, and raise their young. During this time, many thousands live together in breeding areas called *rookeries*. Penguins have loud voices, so rookeries are very noisy places!

There are 18 kinds of penguins. The largest is the emperor penguin, which may stand 1.2 meters (4 feet) tall and weigh 27 kilograms (60 pounds) or more.

Emperor penguins breed in the coldest part of the world at the coldest time of the year. A female lays just one egg. A male keeps the egg warm by holding it on the tops of his feet, under the lower belly. To keep themselves warm, the male penguins huddle close together and walk slowly with the wind at their backs. As many as 5,000 male emperor penguins will huddle together, each moving slowly and carrying an egg on its feet. They do this for two months—without eating!

Like emperor penguins, male king penguins carry a single egg on their feet. But other penguins lay two eggs in nests. Usually, only one hatches or only one chick survives, since it takes both parents to feed just one chick. The chicks are born gray or brown. When they get their black-and-white feathers, they leave the nest and begin to swim in the cold sea. There they must begin to catch food for themselves.

Penguins live only in the southern hemisphere—in Antarctica and on the shores and islands off South America, Australia, New Zealand, and South Africa. Most penguins live in places that get very, very cold in winter. Two features protect the birds from the freezing temperatures—a dense covering of feathers and a thick layer of fat called *blubber* that is under the skin.

The northernmost penguin lives in the Galápagos Islands of South America, near the equator. Galápagos penguins can survive in such a warm climate because cold water flows there from Antarctica. When out of the water, Galápagos penguins spend much of the time in cool caves.

The Adèlie penguin, shown here with two chicks, lives in Antarctica.

penicillin

Penicillin is an antibiotic drug that is used to treat infections caused by many kinds of bacteria. The penicillin stops the bacteria from growing and reproducing. Diseases such as pneumonia and scarlet fever can be cured with penicillin. Infections of the throat and ears are treated with penicillin, too. (*See* **bacteria.**)

Most people can safely take penicillin. But some people are *allergic* to penicillin—they get a rash or fever from it. Others may develop such serious problems from penicillin that they cannot take this drug at all.

Penicillin was discovered in 1928 by Alexander Fleming, a British scientist. By accident, he discovered that penicillin molds prevent the growth of bacteria. During the next 20 years, scientists learned how to separate penicillin from the penicillin mold. They also learned how to produce large quantities of the drug. (*See* **mold** and **Fleming, Sir Alexander.**)

In the 1940s, doctors began using penicillin to treat many diseases. It cured diseases that doctors once thought could not be cured. Penicillin was called a "miracle drug."

See also **antibiotic.**

peninsula

A peninsula is a body of land almost completely surrounded by water. It is attached to a much larger body of land, such as an island or continent. Often, a peninsula is connected to the mainland by a narrow land bridge called an *isthmus.*

North America has several large peninsulas. Much of the state of Florida is a large, flat peninsula that extends into the Atlantic Ocean. Alaska has two large peninsulas—the Seward and Alaska peninsulas. Even larger are Baja California, on the west coast of Mexico, and the Yucatán Peninsula, on Mexico's east coast.

Many European countries are on peninsulas. Italy is on the mountainous Apennine Peninsula. The Balkan Peninsula contains Greece, Albania, Bulgaria, and parts of Turkey and Yugoslavia. Spain and Portugal are

San Francisco (arrow) is on the tip of a peninsula—there is water on three sides.

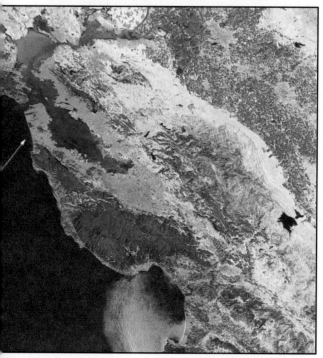

on the Iberian Peninsula, between the Mediterranean Sea and the Atlantic Ocean. Norway and Sweden share the Scandinavian Peninsula, and Denmark is on the Jutland Peninsula.

Asia, too, has long peninsulas. The volcanic Kamchatka Peninsula reaches south from Siberia in northern Asia toward Japan. The Korean Peninsula stretches south from China. Much farther south is the longest Asian peninsula—the Malay Peninsula. It contains parts of three countries—Burma, Thailand, and Malaysia.

Penn, William

William Penn was the founder of the colony of Pennsylvania, which later became a state in the United States. Penn was an Englishman. He was also a member of the Society of Friends—a Christian group often called the Quakers. He hoped Pennsylvania would be a place where Quakers and others could follow their religious beliefs in peace.

Penn was born in 1644 to a wealthy and powerful family. He became a Quaker as a young man. The English government believed that Quakers were dangerous, and made Quaker meetings illegal. Penn was arrested for preaching and writing about Quakerism.

King Charles II owed Penn's father a large debt. After his father died, Penn asked the king to grant him land in America to pay the debt. The king agreed, and in 1682, Penn sailed to America. The new colony was called Pennsylvania, which means "Penn's woods."

Penn set up a government that allowed freedom of religion. He also drew up a plan for a new city, Philadelphia—meaning "City of Brotherly Love." Quakers and others soon came from England and other parts of Europe. They felt safe in Pennsylvania.

Penn stayed in the new colony for only a few years. Later, in England, he fell into debt and served time in prison. He died in 1718.

See also **Philadelphia; Pennsylvania;** and **Quakers.**

Pennsylvania

Capital: Harrisburg
Area: 45,308 square miles (117,348 square kilometers) (33rd-largest state)
Population (1980): 11,864,720 (1985): about 11,853,000 (4th-largest state)
Became a state: December 12, 1787 (2nd state)

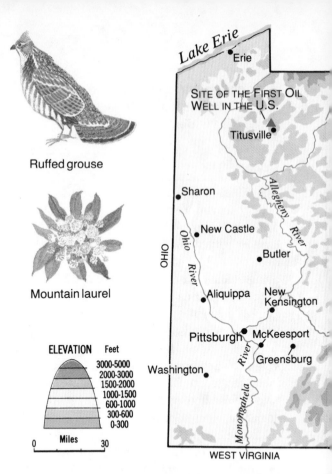

Ruffed grouse

Mountain laurel

ELEVATION Feet
3000-5000
2000-3000
1500-2000
1000-1500
600-1000
300-600
0-300

Miles
0   30

WEST VIRGINIA

Pennsylvania is one of the leading mining and manufacturing states of the United States. It was one of the original 13 colonies.

Pennsylvania, in the northeastern United States, is bordered on the north by New York and Lake Erie. New York and New Jersey are on the east. On the south are Delaware, Maryland, and West Virginia. To the west are Ohio and West Virginia.

Land Almost all of Pennsylvania is mountainous. In the west and northeast, there are beautiful rolling hills. Pennsylvania has much rich farmland. The most fertile soils are in the southeast, in the Susquehanna River valley, and in the northwest, near Lake Erie. Forests cover half the state.

Pennsylvania usually has hot summers and cold winters. The state receives about 42 inches (107 centimeters) of rain every year.

History The first permanent settlement in what is now Pennsylvania was started by a group of Swedes in 1643. Called New Sweden, it was taken over by the Dutch in 1655. The English captured it in 1664.

In 1681, the king of England gave part of the area to William Penn, a Quaker. Penn offered Quakers and others a place to practice their religion freely. The colony he started was named Pennsylvania—meaning "Penn's woods." (*See* **Penn, William.**)

During the French and Indian War (1754 to 1763), Pennsylvania was the scene of much fighting. Later, from 1775 to 1787, the colony played a major role in the American Revolution. The Declaration of Independence was signed in Philadelphia in 1776. The U.S. Constitution was written there in 1787. (*See* **Philadelphia.**)

After the Revolution, Pennsylvania continued to grow. The first oil well in the United States was drilled in northwestern Pennsylvania in 1859.

Many Pennsylvanians were early leaders in the fight against slavery. The state entered the Civil War (1861 to 1865) on the Union side. One of the most important battles of the war was fought at Gettysburg, Pennsylvania. (*See* **Gettysburg.**)

Corn and other grains, used mostly to feed livestock, are Pennsylvania's chief crops. The state is best known for its mining and manufacturing. It is the nation's leading producer of steel and pig iron (a crude iron), and a major producer of coal. Tourism is an important industry in Pennsylvania. Its historical landmarks and beautiful scenery attract people from around the world.

PENNSYLVANIA

PENNSYLVANIA STATE UNIVERSITY

▲ State College

Williamsport

Kingston
Scranton
Wilkes-Barre

DELAWARE WATER GAP

Delaware River

NEW JERSEY

ALLEGHENY MOUNTAINS

APPALACHIAN MOUNTAINS

Susquehanna River

Hazleton

Altoona

Juniata River

Johnstown

Pottsville

Bethlehem
Easton
Allentown

Lebanon

SITE OF THE FIRST PHARMACY IN THE U.S.

WASHINGTON CROSSING HISTORICAL PARK

Harrisburg ★

Reading

New Hope

SITE OF THE BATTLE OF GETTYSBURG AND OF LINCOLN'S GETTYSBURG ADDRESS

PENNSYLVANIA DUTCH COUNTRY

Lancaster

York

Norristown
Levittown

VALLEY FORGE HISTORICAL PARK

Philadelphia

Chester

DEL.

SITE OF LIBERTY BELL, INDEPENDENCE HALL, AND BETSY ROSS HOUSE

MARYLAND

Gettysburg

▲ Historical Sites and Points of Interest

In Pittsburgh, the Allegheny and Monongahela rivers meet to form the Ohio.

People Some Pennsylvanians are descended from the early settlers. Many more are descended from people who emigrated from Europe in the 1800s and early 1900s.

Some Pennsylvanians are called "Pennsylvania Dutch." They are actually descendants of Germans—*Deutsch*—who settled in Pennsylvania in the 1600s and 1700s.

Another group of people, the Amish, live mostly in Lancaster County. Many are very successful farmers, though they use no modern farm technology or machines. Known as the "plain people," the Amish have a community life closely tied to their religion. The Amish dress in the style of the 1700s and use horse-drawn buggies for transportation.

More than two-thirds of Pennsylvania's people live in or near the cities. Philadelphia, in southeastern Pennsylvania, is the state's largest city and the fourth-largest city in the United States. Pittsburgh, the state's second-largest city, is a steel-manufacturing center in the western part of the state. Harrisburg, in south-central Pennsylvania, is the state capital.

29

The mockingbird can imitate the songs of other birds.

perching birds

Perching birds have feet that can hold on to tree branches, telephone wires, and other perches. Each foot has four toes. Three long toes point forward, and one shorter toe points backward. The bird wraps its toes around a perch and locks them in position. The feet hold on so securely that the bird can sleep while perching, even when it is stormy and windy.

Perching birds have feet that can grasp a tree branch.

Altogether, there are 5,500 kinds of perching birds—more than half of all known kinds of birds. Most are small or medium-size. Crows and ravens are the largest. They may be 60 centimeters (24 inches) long. One large perching bird, the lyrebird, may be more than 100 centimeters (40 inches) long altogether. But about 75 centimeters (29 inches) of this length is its tail.

Perching birds come in many colors. For example, wrens and larks are gray-brown.

They blend into their surroundings, making it difficult for their enemies to see them. Some other perching birds are very colorful. Often, the males are much more colorful than the females. For example, the male Northern oriole is black with a bright orange rump and breast and a white band across each wing. The female Northern oriole has olive-colored feathers on the upper body and yellowish feathers on its rump and underside.

Where They Live Perching birds live everywhere except the polar regions. Each kind of bird has its own environment. Some live in low deserts, others on high mountains. Some live only in the tropics, while others live in temperate lands. Those that live in places with cold winters usually migrate to warmer lands for the winter, especially if they are insect-eaters. The birds could survive the cold weather, but there would not be enough insects to eat during that time. (*See* **migration**.)

Many perching birds have successfully adapted to human environments. They live in cities, towns, and on farms. People encourage these birds to live close to them by feeding them. They scatter seeds, crumbs, and other food and fill birdbaths with water.

Perching birds often gather into groups called *flocks*. Some flocks are very big. A flock of crows may have more than 20,000 birds! The crows scatter during the daytime to feed, then gather at night to sleep.

What They Eat Different kinds of perching birds may have very different diets. Some, like crows, eat almost anything. Others can eat only one or two kinds of food.

The birds use their bills to get food. Usually, you can tell what a bird eats by looking at the shape of its bill. A cardinal has a large, heavy bill. The bill is strong enough to crush the seeds that make up the cardinal's diet. The shrike has a sharp, hooked bill for catching small birds, insects, mice, and snakes. The crossbill has a heavy bill that crosses at the tip. This is useful in opening pine cones and removing the seeds.

evening grosbeak

black-capped chickadee

red crossbill

These bills help the birds crack heavy seeds (above), open pine cones (left), or dig for insects (right).

Perching birds help keep the *balance of nature*—a system of natural controls that keep one kind of living thing from overwhelming all the others in any given place. Perching birds eat huge amounts of insects, garbage, and dead animals. But some are nuisances to people because they eat crops and newly planted seeds.

Beautiful Songs Most birds can make sounds. But it is the songbirds that produce the most beautiful calls and songs. All of the songbirds are perching birds. Birds have a vocal organ called the *syrinx.* The syrinx is at the lower end of the windpipe. Inside the syrinx are thin *membranes*—soft sheets of tissue. When air leaves the lungs, it passes over the membranes and makes them *vibrate*—move back and forth very quickly. The vibration of these membranes produces the song.

Each kind of songbird has its own songs. If you watch and listen, you can learn to recognize songbirds by their songs. Some songbirds are named after the song they sing. The chickadee sings "chick-a-dee" or "chick-a-dee-dee-dee." The eastern phoebe calls "fee-be, fee-be, fee-be."

Songs have several important uses, and usually a bird has different songs for different purposes. A bird may sing to tell other birds that it is in the neighborhood. It may sing to tell others, "This is my territory!" It may sing to warn of danger. It may sing to attract a mate.

Some birds can imitate the songs of other birds and even the sounds made by other animals. The catbird has a lovely song, but it sounds like an angry cat when an outsider enters its territory. A mockingbird can imitate everything from woodpeckers to tree frogs. The talking mynah bird can be taught to whistle and imitate human speech. Crows, too, can be taught words.

Mating and Reproduction When it is time to mate, some perching birds perform a courtship dance or song. Usually, this is done by the male to attract a female. For example, the male bowerbird of Australia builds a bower—an archway—of twigs. He decorates the bower with flowers, berries, and other colorful objects. The color attracts the female to the bower.

After birds court and mate, they build a nest. Sometimes, both parents build the nest and raise the young. In other cases, the female makes the nest and raises the young by herself.

Young perching birds are born helpless. They must be kept warm and fed. Before feeding a baby bird, a parent bird swallows the food. Many partly digest it. Then it spits up the food and forces it down the baby's throat. Soon, the baby bird grows feathers, and learns to fly and find food.

The male bowerbird is decorating a "bower" to attract a female at mating time.

perching birds

eastern
bluebird

black-capped
chickadee

white-breasted
nuthatch

Berwick's
wren

bohemian
waxwing

American
crow

American
robin

cardinal

blue jay

cliff
swallow

starling

Well-Known Perching Birds   The following are among the most familiar perching
birds in North America.

Bluebirds Not all birds that are blue are
bluebirds. You can spot a bluebird by its red
breast. The female has duller colors than the
male. Bluebirds build their nests in holes in
trees or in birdhouses built by people. They
eat many insects.

Cardinals The male cardinal is red except
for black around its red bill. The female is
reddish brown with a red bill. Both have
crests of feathers on their heads. Cardinals
eat seeds and will happily use bird feeders
placed in gardens.

Chickadees These are small, plump birds.
They have a cap of dark feathers on top of
the head and a dark bib on the throat. Chickadees spend much of the day looking for
seeds, fruit, and insects. A single chickadee
may eat as many as 500 caterpillars in one
day! Chickadees are friendly birds and can
be trained to take food from a person's hand.

Crows and Ravens These two large birds
with black feathers are related. Crows are
smaller and make a cawing sound, while
ravens croak. They both eat all kinds of food,
including crops, insects, small animals, and
the eggs and young of other birds. They usually live in large flocks. They are the most intelligent of all birds.

Jays The Canada jay and the blue jay belong to this group. The blue jay has bright
blue feathers covering its back and the tops
of its wings. Whitish feathers are on its underside. On its head is a crest of feathers.
Like its relatives, the crows, blue jays eat
many kinds of foods.

Mockingbirds These birds are famous for
their ability to imitate other birdsongs. Scientists who studied one mockingbird found
that it imitated 32 kinds of birds during ten
minutes of singing! Mockingbirds also have
their own beautiful song.

Nuthatches These are small, lively birds.
The *hatch* in their name comes from a word
meaning "hack." A nuthatch wedges seeds
and nuts into cracks in tree bark, and then
hacks away at them to get at the soft insides.
Nuthatches are good climbers, easily moving
up and down the trunk of a tree.

Robins The robin has grayish brown
feathers and an orange-red breast. The female is duller in color. Its song says, "Cheerily, cheerily." Robins eat earthworms,
berries, and insects. They often build their
nests in gardens near people's homes.

Starlings Most perching birds hop about
when they are on the ground. Starlings walk
or run. These birds have dark, shiny feathers and a yellow bill. They eat all kinds of
foods but prefer insects and fruit. They are
noisy birds and often gather together in
huge flocks. Some starlings, such as the mynah bird, can imitate people's voices. Like a
parrot, a mynah can be taught to speak.

Swallows These are small insect-eating
birds. They are excellent fliers and spend a
lot of time in the air. But they are not very
good walkers, because their legs are very
short. They have dark, shiny feathers. Males
and females usually look alike. Swallows
often build their mud nests on buildings or
in birdhouses.

Thrushes Thrushes are medium-size
songbirds. They make their homes in forests, fields, parks, and gardens. They feed
mostly on insects. Some, like the hermit
thrush and the nightingale, have lovely
songs. Bluebirds and robins are kinds of
thrushes.

Waxwings These birds get their name
from small, red, waxy growths on the tips of
some of the wing feathers. Waxwings eat
cherries, mulberries, and other fruit. They
often travel and feed in flocks. Their call
sounds like a weak whistle.

Wrens These are small brown birds with
lots of energy. They have short tails, which
they usually hold straight up or tilted forward over the back. Male wrens have lovely
songs, but the females seldom sing. One of
the best-known kinds is the house wren. It is
a friendly and curious bird that often lives
around houses.

See also **bird** and **animal homes.**

percussion instrument, *see* musical instrument

perfume

Perfume is a substance used to make people, places, and things smell good. Many perfumes are liquids or creams that people put on their skin. Bath soaps, air fresheners, makeup, deodorants, laundry products, and many other things contain perfumes.

Ancient peoples used perfumes found in nature for religious ceremonies. Perfumes are still used this way in some religions.

bay leaf

rose

musk deer

ginger root

lemon

cedar

Perfumes may have both plant and animal ingredients.

Essential oils from flowers, leaves, roots, bark, fruit, plant gums, and spices provide the beautiful smells in expensive perfumes. Animal products are used, too, as *fixatives* —to make the scent last longer. *Musk* comes from a gland in male musk deer. *Ambergris* comes from the sperm whale. *Civet* comes from an animal called a civet cat.

Some perfumes today use artificial scents and fixatives. These perfumes are less expensive and often smell natural.

Most perfumes are mixtures, or blends. *Cologne* has small amounts of essential oils mixed with alcohol and water. *Toilet water* has even smaller amounts. Cologne and toilet water may smell as good as perfume, but the scent is not as strong and does not last as long.

See also **cosmetics.**

Persia

Persia was one of the great powers of the ancient world. It was centered in the area that is now Iran.

The early Persians lived in western Asia, north of the Persian Gulf. Around 550 B.C., a strong leader named Cyrus the Great became their ruler. Under Cyrus, Persian armies moved outward from their homeland and began conquering nearby regions. They were so skilled with the bow and arrow that their enemies could not get near them. Within a few years, Persian kings ruled a vast area. It stretched from Egypt and present-day Turkey to the Indus River of what is now Pakistan. Two later rulers, Darius the Great and his son Xerxes, both tried to capture Greece, but failed. Persia remained a great power until the 300s B.C., when it was conquered by the Greeks.

The Persians divided their empire into provinces. Each province was ruled by a local governor. They treated the people they conquered fairly well, permitting them to follow their own religion as long as they obeyed Persian laws.

The Persians were the first people of the ancient world to make good use of horses for transportation and communication. They had a postal system and built underground irrigation canals. They had one of the first money systems based on minted coins.

The Persians followed a religion called Zoroastrianism. Its founder was a prophet named Zoroaster. He taught that there was a great struggle between the powers of good and evil. This struggle would end with the coming of a savior, who would judge both the living and the dead. Zoroastrian beliefs influenced Judaism and Christianity. (*See* **Christianity** and **Judaism.**)

Persian culture was lively and creative. Early rulers built two great capitals, one at Susa and one at Persepolis. The buildings are in ruins today, but the remaining stone columns, walls, and carvings are impressive. Later, Persian artists became known for

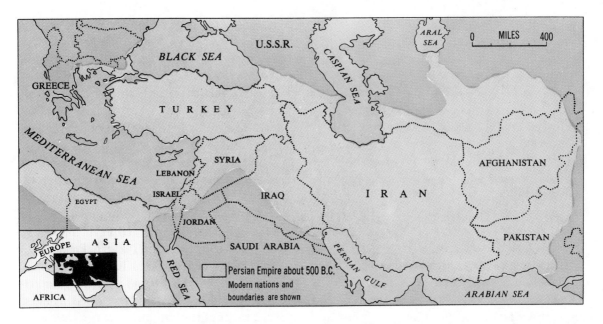

their beautiful, jewellike paintings. Pottery workers made fine tiles to cover walls and domes. Women and girls wove beautiful carpets that took years to complete.

Persian writers wrote mostly about society and religion. The *Shah Nameh* (*Book of Kings*) tells the history of Persia from its ancient days until the coming of Islam in the 600s. The *Rubaiyat* is a collection of verses by Omar Khayyám, a mathematician who lived around the year 1000. These poems are still popular today.

The stone figures along this stairway were carved by Persian artists in the capital city of Persepolis around 400 or 500 B.C.

Peru

Capital: Lima
Area: 496,222 square miles (1,285,215 square kilometers)
Population (1985): about 19,698,000
Official languages: Spanish and Quechua

Peru is a large nation in northwestern South America. It is nearly twice the size of the state of Texas. For three centuries, from the 1200s to the 1500s, Peru was the center of the great Inca civilization.

Peru shares borders with Ecuador, Colombia, Brazil, Bolivia, and Chile. On the west, it faces the Pacific Ocean. The narrow coastal region receives less than 2 inches (5 centimeters) of rain a year. But streams bring water from the Andes Mountains and turn parts of this desert into fertile farmland.

The Andes Mountains cross central Peru. They are the highest mountains in the Americas. Several peaks in Peru are higher than 20,000 feet (6,000 meters). Peru lies just south of the equator and has a tropical climate. But the mountains are so high that many remain snowcapped most of the year.

East of the Andes is an area called the *selva*. It includes the eastern foothills of the

An Indian mother with a child on her back. Most Peruvians are descendants of Indians.

Andes and the edge of the Amazon River Basin. It receives more than 100 inches (250 centimeters) of rain a year. Rain forests and jungles cover the selva.

People related to the Indians of North America moved into Peru about 12,000 years ago. The Inca civilization developed there about 800 years ago. The Inca built cities and roads and made important discoveries in astronomy and agriculture. In 1532, Spanish conquerors led by Francisco Pizarro overthrew the Inca empire and claimed the land for Spain. Spain ruled Peru for nearly 300 years. (*See* **Inca** and **Pizarro, Francisco.**)

In 1821, Peru declared its independence. Since then, Peru has had several constitutions. It has been ruled by elected leaders, dictators, and the military.

ELEVATION Feet

Over 10000
5000-10000
2000-5000
1000-2000
0-1000

0 MILES 200

Today, Peru still shows its Indian and Spanish past. Nearly half the people are Indians. Many more are part Indian. Quechua, one of Peru's main languages, is an Incan language. Most Peruvians speak Spanish and belong to the Roman Catholic church—brought to Peru by the Spanish. Most Indians live in the mountains, and most descendants of the Spanish live in the cities. About one out of five Peruvians lives in Lima, the capital and largest city.

Most Peruvians make their living from farming and fishing. Peru is a leading fishing nation. Peru's other products include copper, iron, and silver.

Peter

Peter was the first of 12 *disciples*—followers—chosen by Jesus Christ to help him. Peter's story is told in the New Testament of the Bible. (*See* **Bible.**)

Before he became a disciple, Peter's name was Simon. Simon was a Jew who lived in Galilee. He worked as a fisherman. One day, while fishing with his brother, Andrew, Simon saw a man walking toward them. This man was Jesus. He called out to them, "Follow me, and I will make you fishers of men." The brothers left their fishing nets and followed Jesus.

Jesus gave Simon his new name, Peter, which means "rock" in Greek. Jesus said that Peter would become the foundation of the Christian church. Roman Catholics believe this meant that Peter was chosen as the first pope. (*See* **pope.**)

Peter traveled with Jesus and shared many experiences with him. He was there on the night Jesus was arrested by Roman soldiers. Peter wanted to fight the soldiers, but Jesus told him to put away his sword.

After Jesus' death, Peter became a leader of the Christian community. He was killed in Rome because of his belief in Jesus. Many people believe that his remains are buried under St. Peter's Church in Vatican City.

See also **Jesus** and **Christianity.**

Peter Pan, Wendy, and her brothers fly off to adventures in Never-Never Land.

Peter Pan

Peter Pan—the boy who would not grow up—is the hero in the play *Peter Pan.* The play was written by Sir James M. Barrie and was first performed in London in 1904. It is about Peter's adventures with three children—Wendy, Michael, and John Darling. One night, Peter Pan teaches them to fly and takes them to Never-Never Land. There they meet Indians, fight pirates, and become friends with a fairy named Tinker Bell.

The pirates are led by Captain Hook. He has a hook in place of his right hand. Years before, his hand was eaten by a crocodile. The crocodile enjoyed the hand so much that it follows the captain everywhere, hoping to eat the rest of him.

Captain Hook tries to poison Peter and capture the children. Instead, he is eaten by the crocodile. Wendy and her brothers return home—without Peter. If Peter goes with them, he will have to grow up. But every spring, he takes Wendy back to Never-Never Land.

Since 1929, money earned by the play has been used to run a children's hospital.

petrified wood

If a dead tree trunk is buried before it rots away, the wood may *petrify*—turn to stone. The petrified wood is then a fossil of the tree. (*See* fossil.)

It is the minerals dissolved in underground water that cause the wood to petrify. The water seeps into the buried tree and carries minerals into the wood. Some of these minerals eat away the wood, cell by cell. Other minerals settle in the empty spaces where the cells once were. As the water leaves, the minerals left in the spaces dry out and become solid rock.

Silica is the most common of these rock-forming minerals. When it dries out, it forms the hard mineral called *quartz*. Silica can take the place of wood cells without destroying their shape.

Petrified wood often has beautiful colors. These come from tiny amounts of other minerals, such as iron oxide—rust—that were in the underground water.

One of the most famous areas of colorful petrified wood is Petrified Forest National Park, in Arizona. There, you can see the petrified remains of trees that died over 100 million years ago.

Over thousands of years, this ordinary tree trunk changed into a beautiful rock.

petroleum, *see* oil; gas, natural

pets

Animals and people have lived together on the earth for thousands of years. At first, people hunted and killed animals for their meat and fur. But before long, ancient peoples developed a different relationship with some animals. People began to tame certain animals and keep them as pets. People have enjoyed having pets ever since.

Pets are our friends. When we are sad, they help us feel better. Pets are fun to play with and teach. Having a pet is a good way to learn responsibility, too. Pets depend on their owners to feed them, keep them healthy, and give them attention and love.

Kinds of Pets People keep different kinds of animals as pets. In the United States, dogs and cats are the most popular pets. Many people like to keep fish, birds, or hamsters as pets. People who live on farms or in the country often make pets of farm animals, such as horses, goats, cows, pigs, or rabbits.

Some people like having exotic pets—pets that are different, unusual, or come from far away. Exotic pets need special care and attention. Snakes and monkeys are two exotic pets kept by some people in the United States. Pets that are unusual in one country are sometimes very common in other countries. Monkeys, for example, are popular pets in some Asian nations.

Wild animals are not usually kept as pets. The bears, lions, and elephants we see in circuses may have been born in captivity. They were probably trained when they were very young. As these animals get older, they can become angry and difficult to control. They can injure the people who work with them.

Small wild animals, such as raccoons and squirrels, are hard to keep as pets. It is their nature to be wild, not tame. These animals are easy to keep when they are babies. But once they get older, they become unhappy and want to be free.

Adults and children bring many kinds of pets to a neighborhood pet show. Animals make good friends for people of all ages.

Though people have sometimes taken in a wild animal that is sick or has been injured, it is not a good idea to try to touch or pet a wild animal. Wild animals are often afraid of people and will defend themselves by biting or scratching. Sick wild animals may carry diseases.

Choosing a Pet There are many kinds of animals that make fun, safe pets. In order to make the best choice, you or your family should ask yourselves many questions. Here are some of them.

Will this pet be comfortable in your home? Large dogs, such as retrievers and setters, like to run and play outdoors. They would be happiest living in a house with a large backyard. Families who live in apartments may be better off with a smaller pet, such as a cat, a bird, or a small dog.

How much time can you spend with your pet? Some pets need more attention than others. Dogs need to be played with, fed, and walked. Cats are more independent than dogs, but they, too, need food and affection. Fish and birds need to be cared for, but require less attention than cats and dogs. It is important to remember that a pet is the responsibility of its owner. The owner must be willing to take care of it.

One of the most important questions to ask is, Do you *like* this particular animal? Choosing a pet should be like choosing a friend. A healthy pet often has a long life. Cats and dogs usually live to be well over 10 years old. Certain birds, such as parrots, may live to be more than 80 years old. Remember that you will probably spend many years with your pet.

Taking Care of a Pet Pets must be fed properly. Dogs and cats usually eat once or twice a day. A large animal, such as a horse, may need to be fed more often. Fish and birds, on the other hand, may go several days without feeding.

A pet needs the right amount of food to stay healthy. Just like people, pets that eat properly look and feel good. A well-fed dog or cat usually has a smooth, shiny coat of fur. A pet that eats too much gets fat and slows down. Overfeeding a pet can be just as bad for the animal as not feeding it enough. Pet foods are available in most supermarkets or in pet stores. They contain vitamins and are designed to give pets a balanced diet.

Pets must also have enough to drink. A bowl of fresh water should always be available for a dog or cat. Water dishes in a bird cage should be refilled regularly. Water bottles for hamsters, gerbils, and rabbits should be checked and refilled with fresh water.

All pets need a place to stay and to sleep. Birds, such as parakeets and canaries, need cages big enough for them to fly in. The cage should have wooden bars where the birds can *perch*—rest. Farm pets, such as geese, need a fenced-in area outside, with shrubs or

A veterinarian listens to a cat's heartbeat during a checkup.

bushes for shade. Dogs that are kept outdoors need a doghouse or a sheltered spot where they can sleep and stay warm and dry.

Cleaning a pet is also an important part of keeping it healthy. Some pets keep themselves clean. Dogs and cats lick their paws to get rid of dirt. Birds clean their feathers with their beaks. But pets may also need help from their owners to stay clean. Brushing the coat of a dog or cat removes dirt, loose hairs, and bugs. Special collars help to keep insects away from cats and dogs. Bird cages and fish tanks should be cleaned out on a regular basis.

Even the best-cared-for pets will sometimes get sick. You should always be alert to any signs of injury or illness. One sign that a pet is sick is a change in how much it eats. Animals normally have good appetites. If a pet is suddenly not interested in food, it might not be feeling well. A dog's or cat's coat may appear dull or matted if the animal is sick. Often, the way a pet acts can signal that it is not feeling well. Animals are like people—if they are unhappy or in pain, they show it.

Sick pets should not be treated by their owners. Instead, they should be taken to an animal doctor—a *veterinarian.* The veterinarian will give a pet the right medicine to make it feel better. Veterinarians also give shots to many pets, such as cats and dogs, to protect them from serious diseases.

Training a Pet Pet owners should teach their pets how to behave both indoors and out. This is important not only for pets and owners to live together more happily, but for the pet's safety. Pets should be taught as soon as possible, because they learn most quickly when they are young. Pet stores and libraries have many books that tell how to train pets.

Training a pet takes time and patience. In order to learn, the pet must trust its owner. As an animal is trained, it should be rewarded for good behavior. Words of praise, a pat on the head, or a small piece of food are ways to let an animal know it has done a good job. When a pet does something wrong, it should be scolded right away. Your pet may not understand your words, but it can understand an angry voice. You might also make a loud noise by clapping your hands or hitting the palm of your hand with a rolled newspaper. It is not a good idea to hit your pet. This can injure the pet and make it afraid of you. Your pet should be scolded only when it is caught in the act of doing something wrong. Otherwise, it will not know what it has done to upset you.

The first part of training a cat or a dog is to make sure it is housebroken. Cats that live indoors need a tray filled with a kind of clay called *litter*. The cat uses the litter box as a bathroom. Cats that can go outdoors usually find sand or dirt to use as a bathroom. Puppies should be trained to wait until they are outside before going to the bathroom. Puppy owners must be sure they take their pets outside after meals, naps, or playtime.

A dog should be taught to *heel*—walk beside its owner. This is important to keep the dog away from traffic and to prevent fights with other dogs. It also helps the owner keep the dog away from strangers, who may startle or upset the animal.

Many people enjoy teaching their pets how to do tricks. Some kinds of birds can be taught how to say a few words or rest on a person's hand. Dogs are often taught to roll over, beg, or "shake hands." Not all pets are easy to train. Cats, for example, are usually not interested in performing many tricks.

People often train their pets to do a job. Dogs are loyal and protective of their owners. Because of this, many people train them to be watchdogs. Dogs such as retrievers and setters are trained to help their owners hunt. Collies and sheepdogs are good at herding cattle. German shepherds and retrievers are often taught to be guide dogs for the blind.

Pet History The dog is thought to be the first animal ever tamed. Instead of killing their own food, wild dogs found it easier to eat scraps of food that humans had thrown

away. Gradually, they came to depend on people for food. In return, the dogs helped humans hunt and barked to warn them of danger. People soon discovered that other animals could be tamed, too. They began to raise cattle, turkeys, and goats. In different parts of the world, horses, camels, and reindeer were tamed and used to help pull or carry loads. People found themselves enjoying the company of animals for its own sake as well as for its usefulness. Dogs were especially popular. Cats did not become popular pets until the 1600s.

See also **cat; dog; hamsters and gerbils; tropical birds; tropical fish; goldfish;** and **aquarium.**

A pet can be as large as a horse or as small as a tiny bird.

William Penn (top) chose Philadelphia as the capital of the colony of Pennsylvania. The city's historic buildings include the Second Bank of the United States (bottom).

Philadelphia

Philadelphia is the fourth-largest city in the United States and one of the most historic cities in the nation. It is in southeastern Pennsylvania, on the Delaware and Schuylkill rivers, about 90 miles (144 kilometers) from the Atlantic Ocean.

In 1681, the English king granted William Penn, an English Quaker, a charter to establish the colony of Pennsylvania. Penn wished to set up a colony where people could freely follow their own religious beliefs. He chose Philadelphia for his capital. Philadelphia was a Swedish settlement started about 40 years earlier. It had been taken over by the Dutch and then by the English. (*See* **Penn, William.**)

English, Irish, Welsh, and German settlers soon joined the Swedes, and Philadelphia grew quickly. It became a center of commerce, trade, and finance. Its busy port shipped out Pennsylvania's farm and forest products and brought in coal, iron ore, and other raw materials for the city's factories and mills. By the time of the Revolutionary War, Philadelphia was the most important city in the American colonies.

Philadelphia played a major role in the American Revolution. The Continental Congress met in Independence Hall in 1775. The Declaration of Independence was signed there in 1776, and the United States Constitution was written there in 1787. Philadelphia served as the nation's capital for most of the period from 1777 to 1800. (*See* **Revolutionary War.**)

Today, Philadelphia is still a leading center of trade, industry, culture, and education. It has the second-busiest port in the nation. The city's chief industries are metalworking, oil refining, textiles, chemicals, and food processing. Printing and publishing are also important.

A visit to Philadelphia is an excellent way to learn about some important events in the early history of the United States. At Independence Hall, you can see the room where both the Declaration of Independence and the Constitution were adopted. Near Independence Hall is the Liberty Bell, which was rung to announce the adoption of the Declaration of Independence. Also nearby is Congress Hall, which was the official U.S. capitol from 1790 to 1800. (*See* **Independence Hall** and **Liberty Bell.**)

Philippines

Capital: Manila
Area: 115,830 square miles (300,000 square kilometers)
Population (1985): 56,808,000
Official languages: Pilipino and English

The Republic of the Philippines is an island nation in southeastern Asia. It is made up of more than 7,000 islands, but most Filipinos live on only 11 of them. Most of the islands are so small that they do not have names. The two largest islands are Luzon in the north and Mindanao in the south. The capital city, Manila, is on Luzon.

The Philippines were formed by underwater volcanoes and lava. Several of these volcanoes are still active. Volcanic ashes and lava have made the soil rich for farming. The main crops are rice, sugar cane, pineapples, bananas, and tobacco. The ocean provides Filipinos with fish, shellfish, sponges, and mother-of-pearl.

Forests cover about half the nation. Ebony, mahogany, pine, and cedar trees are harvested for lumber. People use the bamboo

Thatched houses in Mindanao are built on stilts to keep them above floodwaters.

that grows everywhere to make furniture and build houses.

People first came to the Philippines about 30,000 years ago. About 5,000 years ago, Malaysians arrived from nearby Indonesia and Malaysia. In 1521, Ferdinand Magellan became the first European to see the Philippines. Another explorer, Miguel López de Legazpi, arrived in 1565 and claimed the islands for Spain. Under Spanish rule, the Philippines became an important trade center. (*See* **Magellan, Ferdinand.**)

By the late 1800s, many Filipinos wanted independence, but Spain sold the Philippines to the United States. The sale was part

of the treaty that ended the Spanish-American War in 1898. The Philippines did not gain independence until 1946, after World War II ended. (*See* **Spanish-American War** and **World War II**.)

Since then, many groups have fought to control the government. In 1965, Ferdinand Marcos became president. The nation's economy grew under his 20-year leadership. But Marcos was a harsh and dishonest ruler. In 1986, Filipinos elected Corazon Aquino as president.

Philippine culture is a mix of the cultures of the many peoples who settled and traded there. Most Filipinos trace their ancestry to the Malaysians. Filipino cooking is similar to that of China and Indonesia. Most Filipinos belong to the Roman Catholic Church, whose teachings were brought by the Spanish. Many Muslims live on Mindanao and the Sulu Islands, in the southwest. Islam, their religion, was brought by Arab traders.

Phoenicians

The Phoenicians were an ancient people of the Middle East. They lived in Phoenicia, a small area along the eastern end of the Mediterranean Sea. Today, this area forms the coastal regions of Israel, Lebanon, and Syria.

Phoenician civilization was one of the great civilizations of the ancient world. Its best-known cities were Tyre, Sidon, and Byblos. Phoenicia's wealth was based mainly on trade.

The Phoenicians were great sailors. In the 1100s B.C., they began sailing their ships all around the Mediterranean Sea. As they traveled, they set up colonies in many regions, including Sicily, Spain, and North Africa. Phoenicians may even have traveled around Africa in the 600s B.C.

Phoenician ships carried goods manufactured for trade. These included glassware, metalwork, and cloth colored with a purple dye made from shellfish. Another prized Phoenician item of trade was wood from the cedar trees of the Lebanon Mountains.

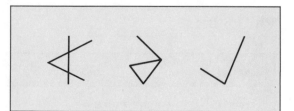

These symbols from the Phoenician alphabet became our A, B, and C.

The most important Phoenician contribution to modern civilization was a written alphabet. This alphabet was later adopted by the Greeks, and then by the Romans. It is the model for the alphabet we use today. (*See* **alphabet**.)

phonograph

A phonograph is a machine that reproduces sound. The word *phonograph* comes from two Greek words meaning "written sound." Record players and stereos are phonographs. Tape or cassette players and compact disc players also reproduce sound, but they are not called phonographs.

Early phonographs played back recorded sounds through a large horn (left). Today's compact disc players (right) reproduce sounds almost perfectly.

Thomas Edison invented the first phonograph in 1877. His invention used a needle to record a voice or musical instrument and then play it back. Voices or other sounds made the needle *vibrate*—move rapidly up and down. The needle's vibrations left marks on tinfoil wrapped around a turning metal cylinder. When a second needle traveled over the same marks, the same vibrations were re-created—and the sound was played back. (*See* **Edison, Thomas Alva.**)

To most people, the machine seemed like magic. It caused great excitement. But there were drawbacks, too. For example, only one copy of a song could be made at a time. In order to make ten copies of a new tune, the musicians had to play the same tune ten times! The phonograph had to be cranked by hand. Depending on how quickly the machine was cranked, the sound might be different. There were no microphones in 1877. When recording a song, a singer had to sing loudly and steadily, so the needle would pick up the vibrations evenly.

Phonographic equipment today has been greatly improved. It runs smoothly on electricity. Recording devices can capture quiet and loud sounds using sensitive microphones. Sound can be stored and played in *stereophonic* form. This means that separate microphones record different sounds. Separate speakers then play back the separate sounds at the same time. This creates a lifelike blend of sounds that seem to come from several directions.

Today, sound is recorded on plastic long-playing records, magnetic tapes, or compact discs read by lasers. Even the most delicate or complicated of sounds can be recorded and played back on modern phonographs and tape players. (*See* **laser.**)

See also **sound recording.**

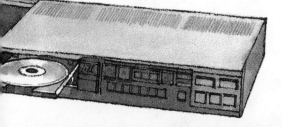

phosphorus

Phosphorus is one of the elements. It is not a metal and not a gas. It is a kind of element called a *nonmetal.* All plants and animals need phosphorus. It helps build bones and provides energy in cells. We get phosphorus from milk, eggs, and plants. Plants get it from the soil.

Phosphorus is found mostly in combination with other elements, especially in phosphate rock. Phosphate rock is treated with sulfuric acid to turn it into superphosphate, a plant fertilizer. Crushed phosphate rock, too, is used as plant fertilizer. In fact, most phosphorus is used as plant fertilizer. There are large deposits of phosphate rock in the Soviet Union, North Africa, Florida, and many Pacific islands.

Pure phosphorus exists in two forms. *White phosphorus* shines in the dark, is poisonous, and burns slowly in air. It catches fire so easily that it can be safely handled only underwater.

Red phosphorus is not poisonous and does not glow. It is made by heating white phosphorus to 250° C (482° F) in the absence of oxygen. When this white phosphorus has cooled, it is red phosphorus. Red phosphorus is used in the striking surface of safety matches. (*See* **match.**)

photocopier

In 1938, Chester Carlson developed a new kind of photography. It was not for taking pictures of people or scenery. It was for making exact black-and-white copies of printed materials. Carlson called his process *xerography.* It let people make quick, dry copies. Another name for the xerographic machine is the *photocopier.*

Today, many photocopiers are *xerographic* copiers, one kind of *electrostatic* copier. Xerographic copiers can copy onto almost any kind of paper. Other kinds of electrostatic copiers need a special kind of paper that reacts to light.

When you make a xerographic copy, a bright light flashes from below on the *original*—what you are copying. The light is reflected back, and an image of the original is focused through a lens onto a mirror. The mirror reflects the image onto a turning drum below. This drum is coated with chemicals that change when they are exposed to light. They form an invisible, electrical picture of the original on the surface of the drum.

The drum is then coated with a thin layer of *toner.* The toner is a powdery chemical that is attracted to the electrical patterns on the drum—the way iron filings are attracted to a magnet. As paper passes under the turning drum, the toner is pressed onto it. Then the paper passes through a heater that permanently bonds the toner to the paper.

Other kinds of electrostatic copiers use sensitive chemicals, too—but they are on special paper instead of a drum. The image of the original is beamed at the paper. Then the paper is passed through toner. The particles of toner stick to the electrical patterns that the light made on the paper.

Today's photocopiers do more than make single black-and-white copies. They can make many copies in just a few minutes. Many copiers have sets of lenses to make copies that are smaller or larger than the original. Most photocopiers have controls for lightness and darkness. Some photocopiers can print colors.

The *laser copier* is the newest kind of photocopier. It works in much the same way as a standard photocopier, but it uses laser light instead of ordinary light. Laser light produces sharper copies with truer colors. (*See* **laser.**)

Today, almost every place of business has at least one photocopier.

photography

Photography is the science and art of using light to make pictures. The word *photography* means "writing with light." The secret of photography is that certain chemicals change when they are exposed to light.

Have you ever looked through a family photograph album? Perhaps you noticed

A photographer got a picture of this monument at night by exposing the film for several seconds. The lights of passing cars look like red and gold streaks.

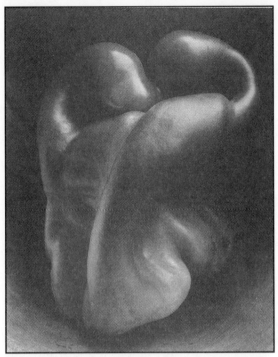

The photographer Edward Weston has made this pepper look like a modern sculpture.

that you or a sister or brother resemble a grandparent, aunt, or uncle as a young person. Perhaps there were snapshots taken on a vacation trip or at a party. Photographs can show us places where we have never been and people we have not met. Years from now, a photograph taken of you today will show what you looked like.

Photographs can show us whole worlds we have never seen before—things we cannot see with our eyes alone. Tiny creatures on a microscopic slide and the rings around Saturn can both be photographed.

History In 1802, an Englishman named Thomas Wedgwood took the first photograph of a person. He coated a rectangular glass plate with silver nitrate, a chemical that is sensitive to light. He had a friend stand sideways in front of the plate, and shined a bright light at him. The light hit the silver nitrate—except where it was blocked by the friend's head. The silver nitrate that was exposed to the light changed, but the part that was shaded did not. The finished photograph showed no details of the friend's face. It was a *silhouette*—a shape with the outline of the friend's profile. Wedgwood's silhouette photographs faded after a time.

The silver nitrate continued to change as the silhouette was exposed to light.

This problem was solved by two Frenchmen in 1814. Louis Daguerre and Joseph Niepce used improved chemicals to coat copper plates that fit into a camera. Their photographs, called *daguerreotypes,* were treated with other chemicals after they were out of the camera. These chemicals "fixed" the image on the plate to keep it from being changed by light afterward. Daguerreotypes were popular, but it took 20 minutes to take a picture. There was also no way to make copies of the original photograph.

In the 1840s, William Henry Fox Talbot made a *negative* using light-sensitive paper. A negative shows the same image as the *print*—the photograph. But where the negative is dark, the print will be light. Likewise, where the negative is light, the print will be dark. Any number of prints could then be made from the negative. In the 1850s, negatives were being made on glass. Soon, photographs began showing up in books and magazines.

By the 1930s, new combinations of chemicals on film made it possible for people to take color photographs. Since then, many other improvements have led to new and better kinds of film.

One kind of film, called *color-reversal film,* is used for taking *slides.* Photographic slides show a *positive* image, just as prints do. But light can still pass through a slide. Slides show very sharp images and can be projected onto a screen.

The Camera A camera is really a box that lets a certain amount of light reach the film inside. When you snap a picture, the camera lets in just enough light to create a chemical picture on the film. (*See* **camera.**)

Motion-picture cameras work like ordinary cameras—but with one big difference. A motion picture camera takes 24 pictures per second. Black-and-white movies were being made by 1900, and movies made from color film were being made by the 1930s. (*See* **filmmaking.**)

Developing Film Once the chemical image is on the film, it must be *developed*. This is done in a *darkroom*—a dark room lit only by a special red light that will not affect the chemicals on the film.

In the darkroom, the film is washed to remove all the chemicals that were not changed by the light when the picture was taken. Then the film is *fixed* to keep the remaining chemicals from changing any further. Now the film is called a *negative*.

Color film uses light-sensitive chemicals, just as black-and-white film does. But color film is made of several thin layers of chemicals. Each layer is sensitive to different colors of light.

Printing Photographs Just as light is needed to expose film in the camera, light is needed to print a picture from a negative. The negative is covered with a glass plate and set under a strong light. The light shines through the negative and then passes through a lens. The negative image is focused onto light-sensitive paper to make the print. A machine called an *enlarger* is usually used to make a larger print from a small negative.

A photographer can make many prints from one negative. By adjusting the enlarger's lenses, prints can be made larger or smaller. The photographer can expose the paper to light through the negative for a shorter or longer time. This controls the contrast of dark and light in the print.

Since the paper is light-sensitive, it must also be fixed to stop its chemicals from changing further. The darkroom protects the paper from being exposed to accidental light until it is fixed.

Instant Photography In 1948, an American named Edwin H. Land invented a new kind of film that could develop itself. Land started the Polaroid Corporation and began producing Polaroid film and cameras. The first Polaroid film was black-and-white, but color film came soon after.

Instant—self-developing—film is made of thick paper that is coated with several layers of chemicals. That is why self-developing pictures are much thicker than ordinary photographs. Some of the layers contain light-sensitive chemicals, like ordinary film. The other layers contain chemicals to develop and fix the photograph. The camera is

Photographers learn to develop their own photographs in a darkroom. At left is an enlarger for making large prints from a small negative.

At left is a black-and-white *negative*—shades of black, gray, and white are reversed. At right is a print made from the negative in which the shades are as we expect.

like a tiny darkroom, protecting the film from accidental light until the photograph has been taken, developed, and fixed. Some instant film starts to develop and fix itself in the camera and then finishes the process out of the camera.

Three-Dimensional Photography *Stereoscopic photography* is a way to make flat photographs look three-dimensional—as if the things in the photograph could be touched on all sides. A stereoscopic photograph must be taken with a special camera that has two lenses instead of just one. A stereoscopic photograph is really two photographs taken at the same time. They show the same images from slightly different angles. When you look at them through a viewer, the two pictures seem to combine

and appear as one three-dimensional picture. Stereoscopic photography became popular before the 1900s and is still enjoyed by children today. You may have a viewer that makes photographs look three-dimensional. You may also have seen 3-D motion pictures created by stereoscopic photography.

Holography is the newest kind of three-dimensional photography. Two separate beams of laser light are used to make the image, which is called a *hologram.* Two other lasers can be used to reproduce it, although some kinds of holograms can be seen in ordinary light. This kind of hologram is sometimes seen on magazine covers, children's toys, or credit cards. If you tilt the hologram back and forth, you can see different sides of the picture. (*See* **laser.**)

A careful photographer exposes film to the right amount of light (center). If film gets too much or too little light (left and right), the picture loses detail and color.

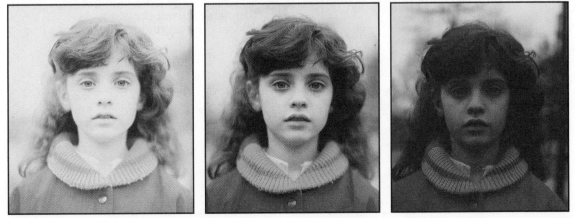

photosynthesis

Photosynthesis is the process that green plants use to make food. The process requires light, air, water, and *chlorophyll*—the green coloring in plants.

A Plant's Food Factory A plant's leaves may be thought of as the plant's main food factory. The leaves of most plants are thin and have a broad surface. The broad surface helps the leaves collect a lot of sunlight. Because leaves are thin, the sunlight can travel to most of the cells inside. The chlorophyll in the leaf cells traps the sunlight and changes it into the energy used by the leaf's cells to make food.

In a plant cell, structures called *chloroplasts* contain the chlorophyll. The chloroplasts of some algae are shaped like stars. Other algae have ribbonlike chloroplasts. The chloroplasts of most algae and land plants are shaped a lot like half a lime. One side is rounded and the other side is flattened. The green chlorophyll in the chloroplasts gives leaves their color.

Tiny openings called *stomata* on the underside of a leaf let air into the leaf. The air contains small amounts of carbon dioxide.

Veins running through a leaf do the same job in a plant that blood vessels do in the human body. They carry liquid to and from the cells. The veins in a leaf are connected to veins in the stem and roots. The veins carry water from the roots to the cells of the leaf.

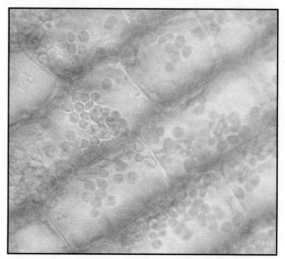

The living cells and chloroplasts of algae are easily seen when magnified 600 times.

How Photosynthesis Works Using the energy from sunlight, leaf cells turn carbon dioxide and water into food. The molecules of carbon dioxide and water are small. Plant cells use the sun's energy to combine these molecules into a large molecule of sugar. Two other substances are produced during photosynthesis—water and oxygen.

The oxygen produced in photosynthesis leaves the plant through the stomata under the leaves. This is the oxygen in the air that we breathe. Some of the water stays in the plant and some of it passes through the stomata. If you have been in a leafy forest in summer, you may have noticed how humid the air is. The air is humid because the leaves release a lot of water vapor into it.

HOW PHOTOSYNTHESIS WORKS

A leaf uses energy from sunlight, carbon dioxide from the air, and water from the ground to make food.

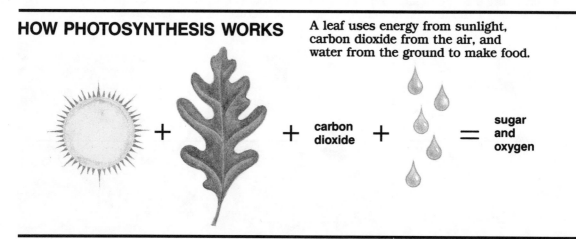

carbon dioxide

sugar and oxygen

The sugar produced in photosynthesis has a lot of stored energy. That is why sugar is an important food. Veins carry sugar to all the working cells in the plant. Some of the sugar is changed into substances, such as starches, that the plant needs to grow and repair itself. The sugar that is not used right away is stored. The plant can use this sugar at a later time.

People eat the parts of plants that store food, such as tubers and roots. The tubers—an underground part of the stem of some plants—are the parts of potatoes and turnips that we eat. We also eat the roots of radishes, beets, and carrots.

Plants make large amounts of sugar by the process of photosynthesis. The leaves of a single full-grown maple tree can make more than 1,575 kilograms (3,500 pounds) of sugar in one summer.

Plants and Light Photosynthesis takes place in two steps. The first step is collecting the sun's energy and changing it so the leaf cells can use it. This step can happen only in the light and is called the *light stage*. The second step uses the trapped energy to combine carbon dioxide and water. This step can take place either in the dark or in the light. It is called the *dark stage* because light is not necessary for it to happen.

Sunlight contains all the colors of the rainbow, but chlorophyll can use only the red and blue light in sunlight. People who grow plants indoors under artificial lights will not

These plants use the energy from artificial light to make food.

have much success with incandescent lights or with ordinary fluorescent lights. Both of them have the wrong color light for plants. Incandescent light is mostly red and yellow. Fluorescent light, the kind usually used in schools and offices, is mostly blue. Special lights for plants have the right mixture of red light and blue light. Plants grow almost as well with plant lights as with sunlight.

Photosynthesis is very important to life on earth. It supplies the oxygen that most living things need to live. It also provides food for all living things. Some living things get this food directly by eating plants. Other living things get this food indirectly by eating living things that eat plants. (*See* **food chain.**)

See also **plant.**

Some plants store the food made by photosynthesis in underground parts of the stem. Turnips, carrots, potatoes, and radishes are stored plant food that people eat, too.

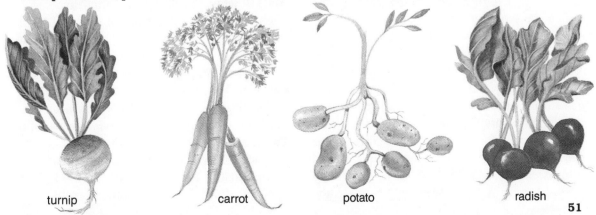

turnip   carrot   potato   radish

51

physics

When a ball rolls over the edge of a table, what makes it fall? When you throw a rock, why does it follow a curved path? Why does the moon go around the earth, and what holds it in place? Why does the light of the sun make things warm? How does the sound of an alarm travel through the air? What keeps an airplane up in the air?

These are the kinds of questions asked by *physicists*—people who study the science called physics. Physicists study the way all kinds of objects—from giant stars to tiny atoms—behave. They also study the forces that cause these objects to move or change. Discoveries in physics have helped us understand our world.

Gravity Modern physics began with studies of basic forces such as gravity. In the late 1500s and early 1600s, Galileo did careful experiments with falling objects. He discovered that light objects and heavy objects fall at the same rate of speed. He showed that the longer the distance they fall, the faster they fall. His experiments were the first to explore how gravity affects everyday objects. (*See* **Galileo.**)

In the late 1600s, Isaac Newton began studying gravity. In one of the greatest of all scientific discoveries, Newton realized that this force kept the moon revolving around the earth, and kept the earth revolving around the sun. The same force that makes

Broadcasting (left) uses laws about sound, light, and electricity. Nuclear power plants (right) apply atomic physics.

a ball fall down from a table keeps the moon and Earth in their orbits. (*See* **gravity** and **Newton, Sir Isaac.**)

The discovery of the force of gravity was important to astronomers. It helped them better understand the movements of the planets and stars. It also helped inventors build new tools and machines that used the force of gravity.

Galileo and Newton worked in other areas of physics, too. Galileo built one of the first thermometers so he could measure heat and cold. Newton studied how light travels and behaves. What he learned led him to invent the reflecting telescope. The study of light —*optics*—became important to physics.

Heat and Energy During the 1700s, people were looking for a kind of energy that would be strong enough to power large machines. Two inventors, Thomas Savery and Thomas Newcomen, had developed steam engines. James Watt made many improvements on the Newcomen engine. He heated water until it turned to steam. Then he used

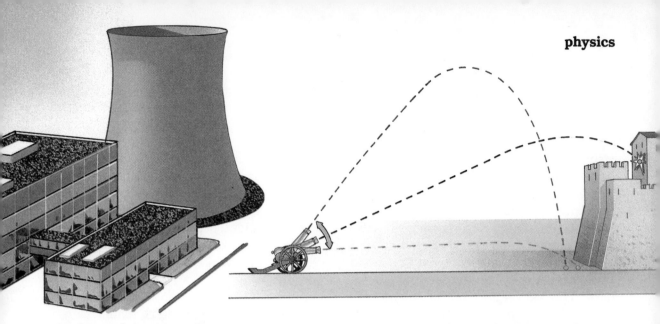

the force of the expanding steam to turn a wheel. Steam engines were soon designed to power boats and trains. Later, other kinds of heat engines were invented to run cars and airplanes. (*See* **engine.**)

Engineers who design and build engines use many discoveries from physics. The laws of physics help predict how much energy will be needed to do a particular job. Other laws show how to change one kind of energy into another. For example, a *pulley* changes a downward motion into a lifting motion. (*See* **machines, simple.**)

Magnetism and Electricity Beginning in the mid-1700s, scientists began learning more about electricity and magnetism. In a famous (and dangerous) experiment, Benjamin Franklin proved that lightning is a form of electricity. He flew a kite in a lightning storm. A metal wire was attached to the kite. A metal key attached to the string sparked when the kite was struck by lightning, because an electrical charge traveled down the wet string to the key. In 1820, Hans Oersted showed that electricity and magnetism were related. A magnet could create electricity, and an electric current could make a magnet. Scientists also learned how to store electricity in a battery. (*See* **magnetism; battery;** and **Franklin, Benjamin.**)

At first, electricity was thought of as a useless curiosity. Then experiments showed it to be very useful. We now use electricity to run engines, appliances, lights, spacecraft,

The laws of physics predict the path of a cannonball and set the aim of the cannon.

and many other things. Today, physicists are working to develop practical *superconductors*—materials that will conduct electricity with almost no resistance. Superconductors may change electronics and other fields completely. (*See* **electricity.**)

Atomic Physics Late in the 1800s, physicists began to study atoms, the tiny building blocks of all matter. Gradually, they learned about some of the things that make up an atom and hold it together. They learned that atoms include *electrons*—the same particles that create the flow of electricity. They also learned that the middle of an atom—its *nucleus*—is held together by tremendous forces. If the nucleus could be broken apart, it would release a new kind of energy—*nuclear power. (See* **atom.**)

In the 1930s and 1940s, physicists succeeded in breaking the nucleus of the atom. An early use of nuclear power was to create nuclear weapons. Nuclear bombs are millions of times more powerful than other kinds of explosives. But nuclear power has important peaceful uses. It can be used to make electricity. Atomic physics has produced many new ways to study and treat illness. (*See* **nuclear power** and **nuclear weapon.**)

See also **Archimedes; Einstein, Albert;** and **radioactivity.**

piano

The piano is a keyboard instrument. It is also sometimes considered a *percussion* instrument. When a player pushes down a key, a hammer hits strings inside the piano. The strings *vibrate*—move back and forth very quickly—making a musical tone. The *soundboard* underneath the strings makes the sound louder and richer.

Unlike many instruments and the human voice, the piano can produce several notes at once. This allows a *pianist*—a piano player—to play the melody and to accompany it with rich harmonies. (*See* **harmony.**)

The piano was not the first keyboard instrument. Long before there was a piano, there were pipe organs with keyboards. Beginning in the 1300s, people were playing on a small pianolike instrument called a *harpsichord.* When a key is pushed on a harpsichord, the machinery plucks a string. This makes the instrument sound a little like a guitar. Another small keyboard instrument, the *clavichord,* was invented in the 1400s. Its strings are struck by metal blades.

The earliest piano was made in the early 1700s. It was called a *pianoforte,* an Italian word meaning "soft-loud." It could play softly or loudly, depending on how hard a player pressed the keys. On a harpsichord, the sound is the same no matter how hard you press a key.

During the 1800s, piano makers learned to build *grand pianos*—large pianos with a long "tail" that held strings. This produced stronger, richer tones. A *concert grand* may be 11 feet (3.3 meters) long—too big for most homes. People usually have smaller pianos—*parlor grands, baby grands, uprights,* and *spinets.* These last two have no tail and fit neatly against a wall.

All the strings in this concert grand piano are visible. Pushing a key (right) forces a felt hammer to hit several strings of the same length and produce a sound.

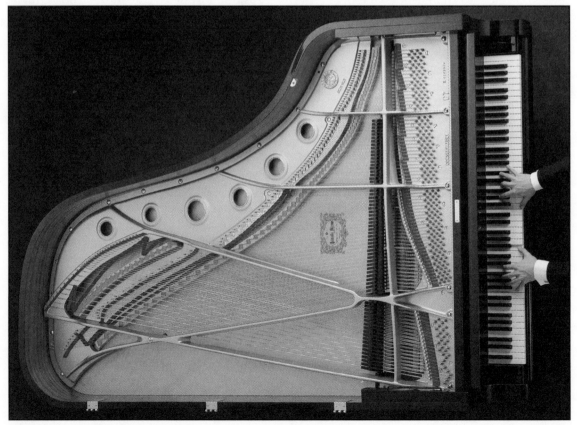

Among the first composers to write music for the piano were Haydn and Mozart. Beethoven and Frédéric Chopin wrote some of the most famous piano music. Later composers who wrote difficult and exciting music for piano were Franz Liszt and Sergei Rachmaninoff. (*See* **Mozart, Wolfgang Amadeus; Haydn, Franz Joseph; Beethoven, Ludwig van;** and **composers.**)

Since then, a great deal of music has been written for the piano. The piano is also used as a solo instrument with an orchestra, or to accompany singers or solo instruments. In a big jazz band, the piano is often used as both a solo instrument and a rhythm instrument. In the United States, many ragtime and jazz musicians played the piano as part of a band. They used new rhythms and harmonies from the music of black Americans. (*See* **jazz.**)

Picasso, Pablo

Pablo Picasso was a famous artist of the 1900s. He did paintings and drawings, but was also a sculptor, printmaker, and book illustrator. He thought artwork should be more than just a picture of how things ordinarily look. Picasso's art showed things in new ways and changed how people thought about art.

Picasso was born in Spain in 1881. His father was an art teacher. From an early age, Picasso showed great artistic talent. At age 14, he began studying art in the city of Barcelona. He continued his studies in Madrid, Spain's capital. He learned to paint the way painters before him had. But after he turned 20, he began to create his own styles.

Picasso's first style is called his Blue Period. From 1901 to 1904, most of his paintings used shades of blue and showed sad, poor people.

In 1904, Picasso moved to Paris and set up a studio. He was very poor at first. After a while, he began to sell his paintings, and he made friends with many painters and writers. For three or four years, Picasso used

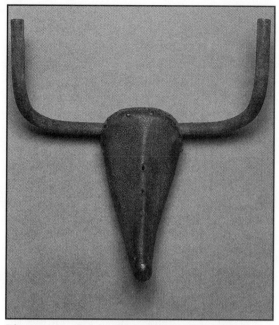

Picasso made his sculpture *Bull's Head* from a bicycle seat and handlebars.

mostly pinks and grays in his paintings. This was his Rose Period. Many of his paintings from this time show circus folk. Picasso also started creating sculptures. In fact, some of the forms in his paintings look like solid, heavy sculpture.

Pablo Picasso in his studio beside a few of his paintings.

From 1907 to 1909, he studied African and Afro-American sculpture. Ideas from the sculptures showed up in his paintings. His people from this period look as though their bodies are built of flat squares and triangles. Their faces often look like African masks.

Picasso's new style became known as *cubism.* His subjects seem to be made of overlapping cubes. You can see both what is inside and what is outside of the subjects. Things in these paintings often look as though they are exploding.

Picasso's styles continued to change. One of his most famous paintings, *Guernica,* was done in 1937. It shows the sadness and horror in the Spanish city of Guernica after it was destroyed by bombs. The huge picture—about 25¾ feet (7.8 meters) long and 11½ feet (3.5 meters) deep—is painted in black, gray, white, and yellow. The people in the painting have open, crying mouths.

Picasso died in 1973, in France. You can see his artwork in museums and libraries all over the world.

Pierce, Franklin, *see* presidents of the U.S.

pig

The pig—also called a *hog*—is a short-legged mammal with a stout body, a big snout, and a short tail. The domestic pig is raised mostly for food, but also for leather and other products.

There are many breeds of domestic pigs. The smallest are miniature breeds that

A pig roots for food. Its ear is marked "41" for identification.

weigh only 27 kilograms (60 pounds) when full-grown. The largest are huge, weighing 360 kilograms (800 pounds) or more. Their rough-haired coat may be black, gray, white, red, or brown. It may be a solid color or patterned with spots or other markings.

Saying that someone "eats like a pig" is usually meant as an insult, but it should be a compliment. Although pigs are not fussy eaters, they do not overeat, and they are not particularly messy eaters.

Pigs have an excellent sense of smell, and they like to root about in soil. A pig pushes the flat end of its snout along like a plow, uncovering roots and anything else in its path.

When you are hot, your body cools itself by producing sweat. Pigs have almost no sweat glands. In hot weather, they cool off by wallowing—lying—in something wet. They prefer to wallow in clean water, but often must make do with a muddy pigsty.

Pigs are among the most intelligent of domestic animals. Some people keep pigs as

Domestic pigs are raised for their meat or their fat. The Chester White shown here is raised for its fat or lard; Hampshire and Tamworth pigs are raised for bacon.

Chester White

Hampshire

Tamworth

pets. Other people train pigs to sniff and root out truffles—rare fungi that grow underground and are highly prized for their flavor. Pigs also can be trained to do tricks, pull wagons, and even swim.

There are eight kinds of wild pigs. They live in Europe, Asia, and Africa. Their bottom canine teeth grow very large, forming two sharp tusks that curve outward and upward. These pigs are fierce fighters, using their tusks to wound enemies. Most wild pigs live in forests. They are active at night, hunting for roots, rodents, and other food.

There are no true wild pigs in North America. Some of the first domestic pigs brought here by Europeans escaped and wandered into the forests. Gradually, their descendants became *feral*—wild again. "Razorback" pigs found in woods of the southeastern United States are feral. There also are feral pigs in other parts of the world.

The peccary, a native of the Americas, looks like a pig but is not a pig. Its tusks grow downward rather than upward.

See also **farm animal**.

pigeons and doves

Pigeons and doves belong to the same family of birds. They live in every kind of temperate and tropical environment—forests, grasslands, jungles, deserts, and cities. They eat mostly fruits, seeds, and grains.

Pigeons and doves are unusual in the way they drink water. They put their bills in the water and draw it up by suction, the way you drink through a straw. Other birds drink by gravity, filling their bills with water and then raising their heads.

There are almost 300 kinds of pigeons and doves. Some are wild, such as the crown pigeon, which is hunted for its beautiful feathers. The most familiar wild pigeons live on city streets. Many people enjoy feeding them, but the pigeons can be a nuisance. Their droppings soil buildings and statues.

Breeding pigeons is a popular hobby. All of the many breeds are descendants of the rock

The common pigeon lives in cities all over the world.

pigeon, or rock dove, a wild bird that lives in Europe and Asia. Some pigeons are bred for show, such as the fantail pigeon and the pouter pigeon. A favorite domestic pigeon is the homing pigeon. It always finds its way home, even from far away. People have used homing pigeons to carry messages from one place to another.

Pikes Peak

Pikes Peak is a mountain in central Colorado, west of the city of Colorado Springs. It rises 14,110 feet (4,233 meters) into the air. It is so tall that it stays snowcapped all year, and trees cannot grow on the upper 2,400 feet (720 meters). It is not the tallest of the Rocky Mountains in Colorado, but it is the most famous. It was the first of the Rockies seen by pioneers coming from the East. During the 1859 gold rush, gold-seekers painted this slogan on their covered wagons: "Pikes Peak or Bust!"

Pikes Peak was named for Zebulon Montgomery Pike, a U.S. Army officer and explorer. He saw the mountain in 1806 and tried to climb it, but failed. In 1820, Major Stephen Long, also an army officer, led a group of men to the top. In 1858, 20-year-old Julia Holmes became the first woman to climb the mountain.

Today, many people visit Pikes Peak to ski and to enjoy its natural beauty. Visitors can ride to the top on horses, on a steep railway built in 1891, or by automobile. The road that ends at the top of Pikes Peak is one of the highest automobile roads in the world. Every summer, the exciting Pikes Peak Auto Race takes place there. The peak also has one of the world's highest weather stations.

Pilgrims

The Pilgrims were English settlers who came to America in search of religious freedom. In 1620, they founded Plymouth Colony. It was the second permanent English settlement in America and the first English settlement in Massachusetts.

In England, the Pilgrims belonged to a religious group called *Separatists.* They were called this because they wanted to separate from the Church of England. English law would not permit this, and so the Pilgrims left England for the Netherlands. They knew that they could worship there as they pleased. In 1610, they settled in the Dutch city of Leiden.

In Leiden, the Pilgrims found the religious freedom they wanted. But they now faced a different problem. Their children were growing up speaking Dutch and learning Dutch ways.

English lands in America offered an answer. In America, the Pilgrims would be able to establish their own community, preserve their English way of life, and still worship as they pleased.

In July 1620, the Pilgrims sailed from the Netherlands to England. At the English port of Plymouth, they boarded an old wine-carrying ship, the *Mayflower*. In late autumn, after a long and dangerous journey across the stormy Atlantic Ocean, the Pilgrims landed in Massachusetts. After signing the Mayflower Compact, by which they agreed to work together as a community, they went ashore and began building their new home. They named it Plymouth Colony.

Soon, winter settled in. The Pilgrims struggled against cold, hunger, and disease. Nearly half of the Pilgrims died, and the survivors grew discouraged.

Toward the end of winter, their luck changed. An Indian named Samoset came to their village. He had learned to speak English from traders, and he offered to help the settlers. Samoset brought his friend Squanto to teach them the skills they would need to survive in Massachusetts. Squanto taught the Pilgrims how to plant corn. He taught them how to spear fish in the streams and to put fish in the ground to fertilize the soil.

That autumn, the Pilgrims harvested a good crop. They also gathered berries and

The Pilgrims found a cold, snowy climate and little to eat. Over several years, they built a settlement of sturdy wooden houses like those below.

hunted game. To celebrate, they planned a great harvest feast, with roast duck, deer, corn bread, clams, and wine made from wild grapes. Pilgrims and Indians sat down together at that feast, the model for our Thanksgiving holiday. (*See* **Thanksgiving.**)

Pilgrim life followed a regular schedule. Each Sunday, everyone gathered to attend a religious service. The service centered around a sermon lasting two or three hours. After the sermon, the Pilgrims went home to eat and to rest, in honor of the Holy Sabbath. In the afternoon, they might return for more worship. The other days of the week were given over to the hard work of running farms and households.

The laws under which the Pilgrims lived were very strict. Some crimes, such as witchcraft, were punishable by death. Other crimes, such as drunkenness or theft, might land the offender in the *stocks.* These were wooden frames built in the village square. An offender's arms and legs were locked into the frame for several hours. The person suffered discomfort and public shame.

Today, a reconstruction of Plymouth Colony allows visitors to get an idea of Pilgrim life. It is called Plimoth Plantation, and each year thousands of people come to Massachusetts to visit it. Anchored nearby is the *Mayflower II,* a copy of the ship that brought the Pilgrims to America.

See also **Plymouth** and **Mayflower.**

pine

A pine is a cone-bearing evergreen tree. Its leaves look like long, thin needles and stay on the tree all year. Its seeds are produced in cones. (*See* **evergreen tree** and **cone-bearing plant.**)

Pine trees can grow where it is cold and dry. They can also survive in very poor soil. For these reasons, pines are often planted in areas that have been burned or damaged in other ways.

There are many kinds of pine trees. *Piñon pines* are small trees that live in the dry areas of the western United States. Indians picked their cones for the seeds, called *piñon nuts.* The *ponderosa pine,* or *western yellow pine,* is a large pine tree used for lumber. The *southern yellow pine* grows very quickly. Its wood is often turned into pulp for paper. In Europe, the *Scotch pine* is an important source of lumber. In North America, it is a favorite Christmas tree.

The oldest trees we know of are pines called *bristlecones.* Some are more than 4,600 years old. They grow in the mountains of the southwestern United States. Over the years, the strong mountain winds have bent these pines into twisted shapes.

Pine trees have many sizes and shapes, and are used for many purposes.

ponderosa pine

sugar pine

monterey pine

pioneer

The first people to explore and develop a *frontier*—a new area—are called pioneers. Pioneers settled the land from the Appalachian Mountains to the Pacific Ocean during the 1800s. They played a major role in the development of the United States.

Many of the pioneers were farm families from New England, Virginia, and the Carolinas. Others were Europeans who arrived at ports on the Atlantic Ocean and then headed west. They were all seeking good farmland.

People packed tools, clothing, dried food, seeds, an ax, and a gun. They yoked a pair of oxen or horses to a wagon and set out. They followed roads that had been cut through the wilderness by woodsmen and by wagons before them. Pioneers traveling along rivers placed their possessions on a large barge called a *flatboat* and floated downstream.

Once they reached the land they wanted to settle, the pioneers built houses. Log cabins were popular in wooded areas. These drafty but sturdy houses were introduced by Scandinavian settlers. Where there were few trees, people built their houses of *sod*—soil held together by roots. When their houses were finished, the pioneers cleared fields so that they could plant crops.

Pioneer neighbors get together to build a log cabin.

Pioneer life was not easy. People worked from dawn to dusk to provide for their needs. They did everything by hand, using simple tools. They raised their own food, wove their own cloth, and made their own furniture. Children did chores, such as planting seeds, fetching water and firewood, feeding the chickens, and milking the cows. It could be very lonely, with no other family for miles around. Sometimes there was also the danger of an Indian attack.

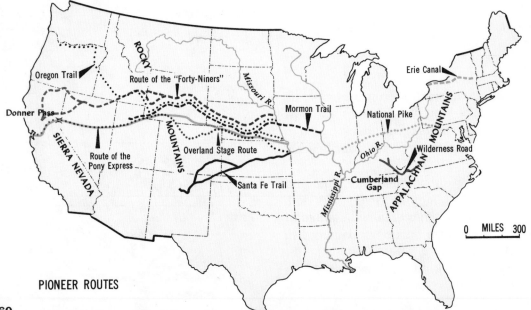

PIONEER ROUTES

a liquid and a finely ground solid. Many pipelines carry oil or natural gas. Others carry water, sewage, coal slurry, and other substances. Pipelines are an efficient means of transportation. Although costly to build, they are inexpensive to run.

The first successful oil pipeline was built in the United States in 1865. Made of wood, it spanned 8 kilometers (5 miles) between a Pennsylvania oil field and the Oil Creek Railroad. Modern pipelines are made of steel pipe. The sections are welded together and then coated to protect them from cracking or rusting. One of the longest pipelines is the Intercontinental Provincial. It runs 4,300 kilometers (2,672 miles) from oil fields in Alberta, Canada, to Buffalo, New York.

Oil and other substances are pushed through a pipeline by pressure. Along the pipeline, pumping stations provide boosts of energy to keep the material flowing. The amount of material a pipeline can transport depends on the type of substance, the pipe's diameter, and the pressure in the pipe. Gases travel at 24 kilometers (15 miles) per hour. Oil travels at 5 kilometers (3 miles) per hour. A pipeline 102 centimeters (40 inches) across can carry about 1 million barrels of oil per day.

The Trans-Alaska Pipeline is off the ground so it will not melt the frozen soil.

Still, the pioneers managed to have fun, too. Sometimes they put work and play together. For example, families would gather for a barn raising. While the men and boys worked to build a new barn, the women and girls prepared food. After the barn was finished, the feasting and dancing began.

Most pioneer children attended school for only one or two months a year. The schoolhouse was usually a single room, with one teacher for all grades.

Many things from the pioneer period have been preserved in museums and national and state parks.

Today's frontiers may be new fields of thought, new land regions, the ocean, or even outer space. There will always be pioneers. It is the frontiers that are different. (*See* **space exploration**.)

See also **Boone, Daniel; Crockett, Davy; California Trail; Oregon Trail; colonial life in America;** and **westward movement.**

pipeline

A pipeline is a system of pipes that carry materials long distances. A pipeline may transport gases, liquids, or solids. Solids are usually in the form of a *slurry*—a mixture of

At the end of a major pipeline, the oil or gas may be pumped into huge storage tanks, or pumped into tanker ships and taken to other places. Some pipelines branch into smaller and smaller lines. The smallest lines carry fuel to individual buildings.

Most pipelines are buried underground. Some go beneath rivers, lakes, and seas. These are covered with concrete to anchor them. Other pipelines—such as the Trans-Alaska Pipeline—are partly aboveground. This pipeline extends 1,293 kilometers (808 miles) from Alaska's oil-rich North Slope to Valdez, a seaport on the state's southern coast. It crosses 20 large rivers, 300 streams, and three mountain ranges, as well as hundreds of miles of frozen Arctic tundra. More than half the pipeline is raised on stilts. If it were buried, heat from the oil inside could melt the frozen soil. If the pipeline lay directly on the ground, it would block the migration of caribou.

See also **gas, natural** and **oil.**

piranha

The piranha is a dangerous fish that lives in the rivers of eastern and northern South America. It has strong jaws and very sharp teeth. When the jaws snap shut, the teeth on the lower jaw fit between those on the upper

Piranhas look harmless, but they attack and eat fish, animals, and people.

jaw. Any animal caught in these jaws has no chance of escaping unharmed.

Piranhas eat mostly fish but may attack anything in their path. They travel in large groups called *schools.* In a few minutes, a school can eat all the flesh off a fish, leaving only the skeleton. Sometimes piranhas attack birds, horses, and other large animals that wander into the water. They will even attack a person.

Adult piranhas are about 45 centimeters (18 inches) long. They range in color from yellow to silvery blue to almost black, and are speckled. The piranha's body is flat, with a sharp spine in front of the fin on its back.

Piranhas are a popular food among some South American Indian tribes. The people also use the fishes' teeth as scissors or razor blades. In fact, some South Americans call ordinary scissors *piranhas.*

pirate

A pirate is someone who steals from ships at sea. Pirates were preying on ships in the Mediterranean Sea 2,000 years ago. In northern Europe, the seafarers known as Vikings carried out pirate raids. (*See* **Vikings.**)

In more modern times—in the 1600s and 1700s—pirates called *buccaneers* sailed the seas around the West Indies and nearby areas of North and South America. They seized silver and gold that the Spaniards were shipping back to Spain from their colonies in the Americas. The Spanish ships were big and slow-moving. Pirate ships were small and fast. It was easy for the pirates to stop and rob the Spanish and then make a quick getaway to one of the many small islands of the Caribbean Sea.

Pirate captains had little trouble finding men to join their crews. Sailors on merchant (trading) ships or navy ships were paid very little, and their lives were hard. Although pirates were not paid, they shared whatever they stole.

Pirates did not sail for any nation, so they obeyed no nation's laws and flew no nation's

There are many stories about pirates who buried or hid great treasures.

flag. Instead, they flew the "Jolly Roger"—a pirate flag showing a white skull and crossbones on a black background.

Some groups of pirates set up small nations of their own. One was on the island of Madagascar, in the Indian Ocean. Another was on the island of Tortuga, off the coast of Venezuela.

Although pirates were usually lawless and cruel, their colorful and daring adventures captured people's imaginations. Among the most famous pirates was Captain Kidd, who was hanged in London in 1701. Edward Teach—known as "Blackbeard"—was another fearsome pirate. He was shot to death in 1718. Stories are still told of treasure that he left buried in Boca Raton, Florida.

Some pirates were national heroes. The Englishman Sir Francis Drake, for example, attacked and robbed Spanish treasure ships in the late 1570s. England and Spain were enemies at that time, so the English queen called Drake a hero and made him a knight. Drake and others like him, who had their government's approval for their actions, were sometimes called *privateers*. (*See* **Drake, Sir Francis**.)

Many stories have been written about pirates. The best-known is *Treasure Island,* by Robert Louis Stevenson. It tells of a hunt for pirate treasure involving a pirate called Long John Silver.

Pizarro, Francisco

Francisco Pizarro was a Spanish conqueror of the 1500s. With only a few men, he defeated the Inca empire of South America.

Pizarro was born in Spain around 1475. His father was an infantry captain, and the boy was raised by poor relatives. He sailed from Spain to the West Indies in 1502. He was with Balboa when Balboa first saw the Pacific Ocean, in 1513.

Pizarro heard about the great wealth of the Inca and decided to search for it. In 1531, he sailed from Panama with 180 men and 27 horses. They landed at what is now Ecuador and spent several months moving down the Pacific coast and into the Andes Mountains. There they met the Inca ruler, Atahuallpa,

Pizarro conquered the Inca of South America and sent their gold and silver to Spain.

and took him prisoner. Pizarro promised to set Atahuallpa free in exchange for a room filled with gold and silver.

The Inca stripped the gold from their temples and even brought Atahuallpa's solid gold throne. Pizarro had the gold melted down into solid bars. But instead of freeing Atahuallpa, Pizarro had him killed.

After Atahuallpa's death, Pizarro took over the Inca empire. He was a harsh ruler and many of the Spanish settlers hated him. One day in 1541, a group of Spaniards surprised Pizarro and stabbed him to death.

See also **Inca.**

plague

Plague (PLAYG) is a contagious disease that used to cause *epidemics*—the rapid spread of disease. During epidemics, plague killed millions of people in many parts of the world.

Plague is caused by a bacterium called *Pasteurella pestis.* This tiny organism lives mainly on rats. It is is carried to humans by fleas. (*See* **bacteria.**)

When the plague germ infects human beings, it causes high fever, terrible headaches, and chills. It often causes swellings called *buboes,* giving the disease the name "bubonic plague." In the past, a person infected with plague usually died within three or four days.

One of the worst epidemics of plague occurred in Europe in the 1340s. Historians believe that it started in Asia and was carried on ships to seaports in southern Europe. Then it spread northward. This epidemic, called the "black death," wiped out a third of the people of Europe.

People who lived at that time left written descriptions of the suffering caused by the black death. One man wrote, "There is such a fear of death that people do not dare even to speak with anyone whose relative has died." According to another writer, some fathers and mothers refused to take care of their sick children.

At the time, no one knew what caused the plague. Many people believed God had sent it to punish them for their sins. Church leaders led the people in prayers asking God to forgive them and spare them. Some people blamed the plague on the Jews. Violent mobs rampaged through the Jewish sections of some cities, killing innocent men, women, and children.

Another terrible epidemic of plague struck England in the 1660s. The Great Plague, as it was called, began in London in 1665. By the time it was over, 65,000 people had lost their lives. At the peak of the Great Plague, 7,000 people died in a single day.

In the 1890s, a French scientist said that plague was a disease of rats and was spread by fleas. After that, it was possible to prevent the spread of the disease by controlling the population of rats and fleas. Plague still exists in some parts of the world, but it can be treated with sulfa drugs.

plain

A plain is a large, flat area of land. Plains occur wherever there is little activity in the *earth's crust*—the earth's outer layer. On the

A sheep ranch on the plains of Patagonia in southern Argentina.

North and South American continents, for example, there are broad plains along the eastern coasts. These coasts are not disturbed by mountain-making forces. But all along the western coasts, the plates of the earth's crust are colliding. These areas are mountainous and have only narrow plains or none at all. (*See* **continental drift.**)

It takes thousands of years for plains to form. They get their soil from eroded mountains—mountains that have been worn down by rain, streams, and rivers. As water rushes downhill, it carries the mountain's rocks and soil, called *sediment.* When the land starts to level out, the water slows down. Slow-moving water cannot carry as much sediment, so the sediment begins to fall to the bottom. As sediment falls, it covers the bumps in the land and fills in hollows. The more sediment a river drops on a coastal plain, the flatter the plain becomes.

Some coastal plains reach far inland, deep into the heart of a continent. In the part of the United States drained by the Mississippi River, the coastal plain reaches over 800 kilometers (500 miles) upstream from the river's mouth. The land there, where Missouri and Kentucky come together, is only a few hundred feet high. But to the north, east, and west, it continues to rise. To the west, it

rises to a vast area of gently rolling, grassy hills called the Great Plains. This dry, nearly treeless area covers parts of seven states between Texas and Canada. The Great Plains' deep, rich soil and dry climate are well suited for growing such crops as wheat and corn. Plains in the middle of other continents —such as the pampas of Argentina and the steppes of the Soviet Union—are also good for this kind of agriculture.

Some rivers have a regular pattern of swelling and flooding after spring rains, and then shrinking again to their normal banks. Each year, a layer of sediment is deposited where the river flooded. Over time, a kind of plain called a *floodplain* is built up. Floodplains have very rich soil that is renewed each year when the river overflows again. People have farmed the floodplain of the Nile Valley for thousands of years. The Mississippi River, too, has created a very fertile floodplain. (*See* **river.**)

planet

A planet is a large, fairly cool object that *orbits*—travels around—a star. All the planets we know about orbit just one star—our sun. Comets, asteroids, and meteoroids orbit the sun, too, but they are too small to be thought of as planets. One star often orbits another star, but this does not make it a planet. Stars are much hotter than planets and give off great amounts of energy.

Early astronomers realized that not all the objects they saw in the sky were stars. The stars seemed to be in patterns called *constellations.* Every night, the unchanging constellations crossed the sky along the same paths. But other objects in the sky seemed to wander among the constellations. These "wanderers" are the planets. In fact, the word *planet* means "wanderer."

The early Greeks pictured the universe as several crystal spheres—hollow balls—each nesting inside the next, larger one. The spheres revolved around the earth, which was at the center of the system. The stars all

Neptune

Uranus

Jupiter

Mars

Earth

Sun

Venus

Mercury

Pluto

asteroid belt

Saturn

The planets in correct size relationship and order from the sun (right).
The planets' orbits are much farther apart than the diagram shows.

had a place on the largest, outer sphere. Since the planets' movements did not appear to have any relationship to each other or to the stars, each planet had its own sphere.

The ancient Greeks knew of five wanderers plus Earth, which they did not think of as a wanderer. Today, we know there are nine planets, including Earth. All nine travel around the sun. They are—in order going out from the sun—Mercury, Venus, Earth, Mars, Jupiter, Saturn, Uranus, Neptune, and Pluto. Slight changes found over hundreds of years in the orbits of Neptune and Uranus have led to the idea that there may be a tenth planet, which scientists call Planet X.

The planets travel around the sun in regular patterns. All these patterns or paths, called *orbits,* are close to the same plane. This means that if you could travel out from the sun in a straight line, you would pass close to the path of each planet. Seen from Earth, the planets seem to wander back and forth. Seen from space, their paths are *ellipses*—slightly flattened circles—that go around the sun.

Planets Around Other Stars Astronomers believe that many stars besides our

sun have planets revolving around them. But this is hard to prove. We have not been able to see any planets around even the closest stars.

In 1987, astronomers found evidence of two planets outside our solar system. They discovered some stars that move slightly. This motion may be caused by a large planet. Astronomers have also found rings or clouds of rocky debris or ice chunks around some nearby stars. These rings or clouds are similar to those we think existed in our solar system before the planets began to form. This makes astronomers think that planets are forming around these nearby stars, and that planets have probably formed around other stars, too.

What Planets Are Like Early astronomers noticed that planets were different from stars in other ways besides their motion. Stars seemed to twinkle much more than planets did. Also, stars always shone with the same brightness, but planets appeared to change in brightness as they moved around the sky. We know now that this is because planets are sometimes closer to Earth and sometimes farther away. When astronomers began using telescopes in the 1600s, they saw that the planets looked like *discs*—filled-in circles—while the stars still looked like points.

Galileo was the first astronomer to study the planets with a telescope. He discovered that the planet Jupiter had moons. He saw the rings around Saturn, although he was not sure what they were. He saw that Venus appeared to change shape the way the moon does, from full—round—to crescent-shaped and back. The planets were not only different from the stars, they were different from each other—in size and in their distance from the sun, and in other ways as well. Today, with a strong telescope or binoculars,

you can see some of the features on nearby planets, such as craters and color patches.

Even though each planet is different, the planets do fall into groups with common features. The four planets closest to the sun—Mercury, Venus, Earth, and Mars—are solid balls of rock and heavy metals such as iron. The core of these four planets may be hot, but all of them have a hard outer surface. Because they are like Earth, the other inner planets are called the *terrestrial* —Earthlike—planets.

The next four planets—Jupiter, Saturn, Uranus, and Neptune—are much larger and are made mostly of gas. They are called the *gas giants*. As far as we know, they do not

THE PLANETS OF THE SOLAR SYSTEM

	Distance from sun km (miles)	Time to revolve around sun	Distance through center km (miles)	Other facts
Mercury	57,900,000 (35,960,000)	88 Earth days	4,878 (3,031)	Nearest to sun. Travels at greatest speed.
Venus	108,200,000 (67,200,000)	224.7 Earth days	12,104 (7,517)	Atmospheric pressure is 90 times greater than Earth's.
Earth	149,600,000 (92,900,000)	365.26 Earth days (1 Earth year)	12,756 (7,921)	Only planet known to have living things. Has 1 moon.
Mars	227,900,000 (141,500,000)	687 Earth days (1.7 Earth years)	6,787 (4,215)	Earth probes visited surface. Has 2 moons.
Jupiter	778,300,000 (438,300,000)	11.86 Earth years	142,800 (88,700)	Largest and most massive. Has at least 16 moons.
Saturn	1,472,000,000 (914,000,000)	29.46 Earth years	120,000 (74,520)	Huge "rings" reach far into space. As many as 23 moons.
Uranus	2,870,000,000 (1,782,000,000)	84.01 Earth years	51,200 (32,000)	Voyager pased by in 1986. Has at least 15 moons.
Neptune	4,497,000,000 (2,793,000,000)	164.1 Earth years	49,500 (30,739)	May be a "twin" to Uranus Has at least 2 moons.
Pluto	5,900,000,000 (3,664,000,000)	247.7 Earth years	2,290 (1,397)	Smallest of all the planets. Has 1 large moon.

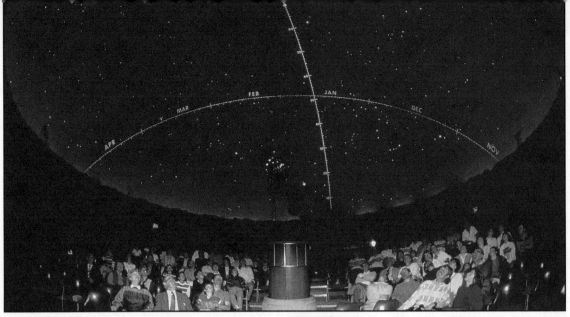

The audience at a planetarium looks up at the "night sky." The stars and planets are projected onto the domed ceiling.

have a hard surface, though they may be solid inside.

Pluto is so far away that we do not know much about it. It seems to have a hard surface, but the surface is probably ice, not rock. Pluto is very small, unlike its neighbor, Neptune. Pluto seems unlike either the terrestrial planets or the gas giants.

See also **solar system; Earth; Jupiter; Mars; Mercury; Neptune; Pluto; Saturn; Uranus;** and **Venus.**

planetarium

A planetarium (plan-uh-TER-ee-um) is a machine that shows how the stars, moon, planets, and other heavenly bodies move around the sun. It shows what you would see if you could spend months, years, or even centuries watching the sky. The machine itself is called a planetarium. The word *planetarium* also refers to the room or building in which the machine operates.

Planetarium machines must be complex to show accurately how all the objects in the heavens move at once. For example, they must be able to show how the heavens appear as the earth tilts on its axis. Computers control the movements of modern planetariums. Some planetariums can even show how the heavens appear from a place other than Earth.

A planetarium is set up in a large room. Often, the room has a domed ceiling and theater seats. The lights in the room are turned off, and a big machine projects small spots of light on the ceiling. These lights represent the planets and stars.

With the lights off and the planetarium operating, you feel as though you are looking up at the night sky. Stars look brighter, and the sun appears dimmer. The planets and other heavenly bodies may appear very large. They are all shown in their correct positions, moving along their orbits. Meanwhile, the operator or another person explains what you are seeing.

Motion may be shown at any speed. The planetarium operator may want to follow the path of a particular planet or constellation slowly. The operator may choose instead to show how the sky looked hundreds of years ago, or speed up the display so you can see the solar system go through its complete 26,000-year cycle. (*See* **solar system.**)

The planetarium was invented in Germany in the early 1900s. Since then, planetariums have been built in many of the world's cities. They are used to train astronomers and navigators. They are best known as places where students and the general public can learn about the movements of heavenly bodies.

See also **astronomy** and **observatory.**

plant

Plants are one of the five major groups of living things. They live in almost every part of the world. They live on land and in fresh and salt water. This entry will discuss only plants that grow on land. To read about plants that live in water, see **ocean plants** and **water plants.**

Plants are made up of many complex cells with cell walls. (Animal cells do not have cell walls.) Most plants make their own food.

Animals could not exist without plants. All animals eat either plants or other animals that eat plants. Plants also supply the oxygen that all living things need to survive.

Plant Parts Most plants have three parts—roots, stems, and leaves. Each part does a job to help the plant live.

Most roots grow deep into the ground, though some plants have roots that wrap around the branches of a tree or shrub. Roots hold the plant in place. Tiny root hairs absorb water and minerals from the soil. The water and minerals flow to other parts of the plant, where they are used to make food. The roots of some plants, such as carrots and beets, store food for the plant, too. (*See* **roots.**)

In its leaves, a plant makes its food by the process of *photosynthesis*. During photosynthesis, the plant uses sunlight, water, and carbon dioxide gas to make sugar. Then the sugar is stored in the plant's roots. Oxygen left over from the process is released into the air. (*See* **photosynthesis.**)

Land plants have special traits that help them survive on land. The plant's stem holds its leaves up to the sunlight. This job is very important because leaves must have sunlight to make food. Most plants have tiny tubes inside their stems that carry food from the leaves to the stem and roots. The tubes also carry minerals and water from the soil to the leaves. These tubes also help it live on land. Land plants have a waxy covering that keeps them from losing water into the air. Plants that live in humid places have only a thin covering. Since the air is moist, they do not lose a lot of water. Plants that live in dry areas usually have thick waxy coverings to hold water inside.

Why Plants Are Green Green plants get their color from *chlorophyll*—a green substance. The chlorophyll is in small structures called *chloroplasts* inside the cells of leaves and stems. Plants need chlorophyll to make food. The chlorophyll captures the sunlight needed to carry out photosynthesis. As leaves die, the chlorophyll changes into other substances. Then you can see the other colors that were in the leaves all along—such as yellow, red, and brown. (*See* **leaf** and **color.**)

Plants are complicated living things that have specialized parts to help them live.

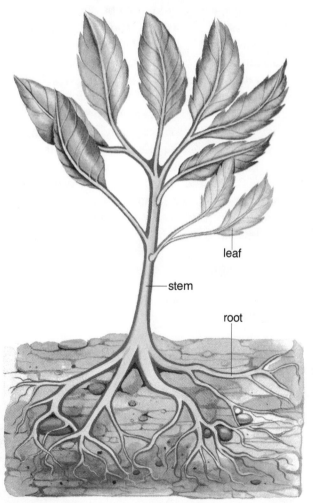

leaf

stem

root

Plants use some of the food they make just to stay alive. They also use some of the food they make to grow and to make flowers, fruits, and seeds. Plants store some of the food in their roots to use later. There are many plants that seem to die down in winter. But they actually use the stored food to survive the winter and to begin growing again in spring. Some plants—such as onions and tulips—grow from *bulbs.* Bulbs are layered, rounded structures that store food for the new plant and protect the plant until it is time for it to sprout. (*See* **bulb.**)

Some plants have green leaves and stems. Most of the parts of these plants can make food. But trees and shrubs make food only in their green leaves. Their stems and branches are covered with a woody bark that gives them strength and protection. Bark cells, however, have no chloroplasts, so photosynthesis does not occur in woody plant parts. The leaves of these woody plants must make enough food to keep the whole plant alive.

Kinds of Plants Trees have a *trunk*—a single, large, woody stem—growing from the ground. Branches grow from the trunk and give the tree its shape. Many cone-bearing trees have long branches growing near the ground. The closer the branches are to the top of the trunk, the shorter they are. This gives the tree a cone shape. Other trees lose their lower branches as they grow. The upper branches remaining hold their leaves high above the ground and out of the shadows of nearby trees. (*See* **tree.**)

Shrubs have several woody stems growing from the ground. Shrubs are usually smaller than trees, have thinner stems, and do not live as long. Many people like to trim shrubs into shapes. Some people even trim shrubs into the shapes of animals!

Vines have long stems that grow along the ground, up trees or walls, or around fences. Vines may be woody, but their stems cannot stand upright by themselves. Many vines have parts that hold them in place. Ivy vines have roots growing from their stems that cling to walls and trees. Grapevines have *tendrils*—strong green threads that curl tightly around anything they touch.

We often use the word *herb* for a plant that is useful in cooking and medicine or that has a pleasant scent. (*See* **herb.**)

But *herb* has a wider meaning. Herbs are plants with soft green bodies. They do not grow hard woody stems. Daisies, petunias, dandelions, and violets are all herbs. *Annual herbs* live for one growing season and die in autumn. Only their seeds survive the winter. *Perennial herbs* live year after year. In autumn, the stems and leaves die down. The roots survive the winter by using the food stored in them. In spring, the perennial sends up new stems.

Examples of four families in the huge kingdom of plants.

cone-bearing

flowering plants

ferns

mosses

The Indian pipe has no chlorophyll—it gets food from other plants.

There are thousands of kinds of land plants. The main groups are mosses, ferns, cone-bearing plants, and flowering plants.

Mosses and liverworts do not have roots, but they do have tiny hairs that hold them to the soil and take in a little water. Mosses and liverworts do not have tubes for carrying materials from one part of the plant to another. Instead, raw materials, food, and water travel from cell to cell. Without roots and tubes, these plants can grow to be only a few inches tall. They often grow in large groups that make a mat on the forest floor. (*See* **mosses and liverworts.**)

Ferns have been living on earth since prehistoric times. We often see only the leaves of this plant. Its stems grow underground. Like mosses and liverworts, ferns do not flower. They reproduce by spores instead of by seeds. (*See* **fern.**)

Cone-bearing plants include some kinds of trees and shrubs. They produce seeds, which develop inside cones. Many of these plants are *evergreen*—they have leaves all year long. (*See* **cone-bearing plant.**)

Flowering plants produce seeds inside special structures called flowers. This group includes many kinds of trees, shrubs, and vines, and all herbs. (*See* **flower; pollination;** and **seed.**)

The group of flowering plants includes some plants that do not behave like plants. Almost all plants make their own food, but a few do not. Dodder and Indian pipe are plants that grow on other plants. They have no chlorophyll, and so they cannot make their own food. Dodder and Indian pipe are *parasites.* They take food from the plants on which they grow. Pitcher plants and Venus's flytraps do have chlorophyll and can make their own food. But they live in places where they cannot get enough nitrogen from the soil. These plants have another, very unusual way to get the nitrogen they need. They actually trap insects in their leaves and digest them. (*See* **flowering plant.**)

Plants provide us with food, fibers, lumber, medicines, perfumes, spices, and many other products. As well as being useful, plants are beautiful. We have created gardens and parks so we can enjoy their beauty.

See the Index for entries on individual kinds of plants.

See also **plant breeding; plant poisons; respiration; plants of the past;** and **botany.**

A Venus's-flytrap catches insects in its leaves. The leaves close when anything disturbs the "hairs" on the inside walls.

plant breeding

If you have ever picked wild strawberries, you know that they are much smaller than strawberries from the supermarket. The difference in size is a result of plant breeding.

Plant breeding began long ago, in a simple way. Early farmers got seed for their next crop by saving seeds from the plants they were harvesting. They saved the seed from their best plants. They might select plants with the sweetest or largest fruit. They might select plants that produced fruit the earliest, or plants that could stand the cold. When farmers planted the seeds from these plants, they got more plants with the same good qualities.

The pollen from one type of tulip is used to fertilize another. The offspring will be different from either of the parents.

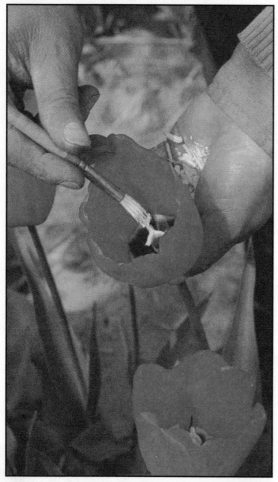

Strawberries that grow in the wild (left) are smaller than those bred by farmers.

Later, farmers learned that they could take pollen from one plant and fertilize the flowers of another plant with it. The seeds that resulted sometimes grew into plants with the good *traits*—qualities—of both plants. (*See* **pollination** and **hybrid seed**.)

Plant breeding has produced green bean plants with different shapes. Some green bean plants are tall vines, and others are short bushes. As a result of plant breeding, tomatoes come in many sizes, shapes, and colors. They may be red, pink, or yellow. Some are large and round, while others are the size of cherries.

The wild cabbage may be the plant that has been bred in the greatest number of ways. By selecting plants to breed for certain traits, people have created a variety of vegetables from wild cabbage. These vegetables include red cabbage, green cabbage, kohlrabi, turnips, broccoli, cauliflower, and brussels sprouts.

Today, plant breeders still get new plants by using the pollen from one plant to fertilize another plant. They also have other ways of creating new plant varieties. Breeders can treat plants with chemicals that change the makeup of the fertilized eggs. The giant strawberries you grow or buy are a result of this process. Using radiation on plants is another way to get new traits in plants. The radiation causes *mutations*—changes—in the plants. The good changes can be used in plant breeding.

See also **genetics** and **heredity**.

plant poisons

Plants cannot run away when they are in danger. How can they protect themselves? Some plants have sharp thorns that stick any animal that tries to eat the plant. Some have coloring that helps them blend into their surroundings. But many more plants protect themselves with poisons. Plant poisons help keep plants and fruits from being eaten. They also may help a plant get the things it needs to grow, flower, and produce seeds.

You probably already know about some plant poisons. Some plants—such as poison ivy, poison oak, and poison sumac—have substances in their leaves and stems that can cause itchy rashes when they come in contact with your skin.

Other common plants have poisons, too—even the plants we use for food. It is important to store potatoes in a cool, dark place. When potatoes are left in the sun, green patches form on the skins. Harmful poisons are made in these green areas, and they should never be eaten. Peaches, plums, apricots, and cherries store small amounts of poison in their seeds. The fruits are safe to eat, but the seeds are not. Rhubarb stalks are used in tasty desserts, but their leaves contain poisons that affect blood clotting. The cassava, a small South American shrub, contains a deadly poison, too. But when the cassava is prepared in the right way, it is safe to eat. In fact, the dessert tapioca is made from cassava.

Many plants that grow from bulbs have poisons in the bulbs. The poisons in daffodil and autumn crocus bulbs keep them from being eaten by mice and moles.

Some plants use poisons to help their chances of getting the things they need to survive. For example, the roots of creosote bushes give off poisons that kill nearby plants. By killing other plants, the creosote gets plenty of space in which to grow and collect water. Getting enough water is very important to the creosote bush, because it lives in places that do not receive much rainfall. Sunflower seeds, too, release a poison that kills other plants. This gives the sunflower seed a better chance to sprout and grow.

Plants can produce poisons in their roots, stems, leaves, seeds, and fruits. Bleeding hearts, buttercups, and star-of-Bethlehem are showy flowers found in many gardens. Yet all are somewhat poisonous. These plants are lovely to look at, but no part of them should ever be eaten.

SOME POISONOUS PLANTS

Peaches and potatoes are good to eat, but peach pits and green spots on potato skins are poisonous.

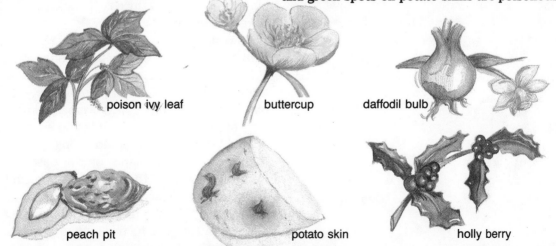

poison ivy leaf   buttercup   daffodil bulb

peach pit   potato skin   holly berry

plants of the past

Fossils of the earliest land plants are more than 400 million years old. These plants were very small and simple. They had stem-like structures but no roots, leaves, or flowers. Scientists divide these early plants into two groups. One group was the mosses, which still live on earth. The other group included the ancestors of today's ferns and cone-bearing plants. The plants in the second group are now extinct. We only know about them from their fossils. (*See* **fossil** and **mosses and liverworts.**)

Mosses and ancient ferns are the oldest plants known to have existed.

horsetail

seed fern

club moss

As plants on land evolved, leaves and roots developed, and plants became larger. By 350 million years ago, there were "forests" of large, treelike plants. Some were giant ferns with narrow *fronds*—leaves—growing from underground stems. Others were seed ferns. Seed ferns had tall trunks and leaves that looked like fern fronds, but produced seeds. Other "trees" were actually giant club mosses. Unlike true mosses, club mosses have upright stems and underground roots. The giant club mosses were up to 30 meters (100 feet) tall and more than 1 meter (3 feet) across. There were plants related to today's horsetails that grew about 15 meters (50 feet) tall. (*See* **fern** and **club moss.**)

Between 290 and 350 million years ago, the horsetails and the giant ferns and club mosses covered much of the earth. Their fossils are found on every continent. Insects, reptiles, and amphibians lived among them.

When these plants died, dirt and other materials covered them. Layer upon layer built up. The weight of the top layers put pressure on the lower layers. Over millions of years, the dead plant matter turned into coal. Coal deposits sometimes contain fossils of these ancient plants. (*See* **coal.**)

Between 195 and 245 million years ago, the era of the dinosaurs began, and the first cone-bearing plants evolved on earth. These plants looked more like today's tree ferns than today's cone-bearing trees. Unlike other plants, they reproduced by seeds. (*See* **cone-bearing plant.**)

Flowering plants are the newest kind of plants. Their earliest fossils are only about 135 million years old—though this is older than the earliest fossils of the mammals and birds we know today. The flowers of this new kind of plant were very simple and were pollinated by the wind. (*See* **flowering plant.**)

We know many plants of the past only from their fossils. Others, such as horsetails and ferns, are present in smaller forms than in the past. Still others, such as the mosses, have changed little in the millions of years they have lived on earth.

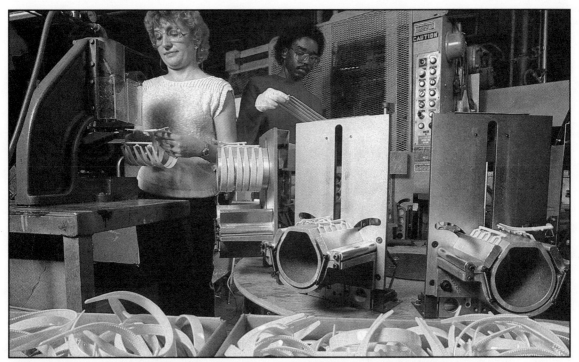

This worker puts straight plastic strips into heater-pressers to form the strips into rounded shapes. The strips are cut apart to make finished headbands.

plastic

Plastics come in countless shapes and colors. They may be rigid or flexible. They may be transparent or solid. Every day, we use many things made of plastic—the buttons on our clothes, our toothbrushes, combs, pens, toys, and more.

Plastics are manufactured materials made of giant molecules. Each molecule consists of hundreds or even millions of atoms. The kinds of atoms in a molecule of plastic can vary. The atoms can also be arranged in many ways. The different compositions and arrangements make possible the many kinds of plastics.

Molecules of plastic often include atoms of hydrogen, oxygen, nitrogen, and silicon. Carbon atoms make up the "backbone" of these giant molecules. Sometimes the carbon atoms join only one kind of atom. Sometimes they join several kinds of atoms. The molecules may be arranged in rows, or they may be connected, forming patterns like connected rings.

Growing a Molecule A plastic molecule can be "grown" by adding atoms to a starting material. Scientists call this starting material a *monomer.* Monomers form plastics by linking to themselves. A string of several monomers is called a *polymer—poly-* means "many." A wide variety of monomers come from petroleum and coal.

Ethylene is the monomer that forms polyethylene, a plastic used to make trash cans. Two ethylene monomers or hundreds can be linked. Scientists grow the molecule to the length they need. Polyethylene's hardness depends on the length of its molecule.

Two Kinds of Plastics Scientists divide plastics into two classes—thermoplastics and thermosetting plastics.

Thermoplastics become soft or liquid when they are heated. They become solid when they are cooled. They can be heated and cooled over and over. Thermoplastics are usually formed into shapes by molds.

Polyethylene is a widely used thermoplastic. It is the material in sandwich bags and tough trash cans. To make a polyethylene trash can, polyethylene is melted and poured into a trash-can shaped mold. The hot, flowing polyethylene fills the mold. When the mold is cooled, the polyethylene freezes into the shape of a trash can. Like other thermoplastics, polyethylene will become soft if it is reheated.

A *thermosetting* plastic starts as a liquid. To set it into a shape, a thermosetting plastic is mixed with a liquid called a hardener. The mixture is then forced into a mold. Suddenly, the mixture of the two chemicals begins to react. The mixture becomes very hot and turns into a rigid, solid shape. A thermosetting plastic cannot be remelted and reshaped, because its molecules are crossed and joined like the lines in a net. When heated, a thermosetting plastic burns instead of melting.

Uses of Plastic Plastics can be easily molded into many products that are inexpensive, lightweight, rustproof, waterproof, and resistant to other chemicals. Most plastics do not conduct heat or electricity well, so they make good insulators. Most kinds of paints and adhesives are made from plastics. (*See* **paint** and **glue**.)

There are many kinds of thermoplastics besides polyethylene. *Polyvinyl chloride* is used for pipes and house sidings. *Polypropylene* is in some carpets and is made into bottles. *Polystyrene* is the ingredient that makes Styrofoam, the rigid plastic filled with air bubbles often used in food packages.

Polyesters and *polyurethanes* are common thermosetting plastics. Polyesters are strong enough to make car and boat bodies. Polyurethanes are used for insulation in houses.

In 1986, the world used 135 billion kilograms (300 billion pounds) of plastics. One-third of this was used in the United States. Thermoplastics made up more than three-fourths of the total amount.

Polypropylene, one type of thermoplastic, is heated and molded to make products such as fan blades, children's toys, and picnic coolers.

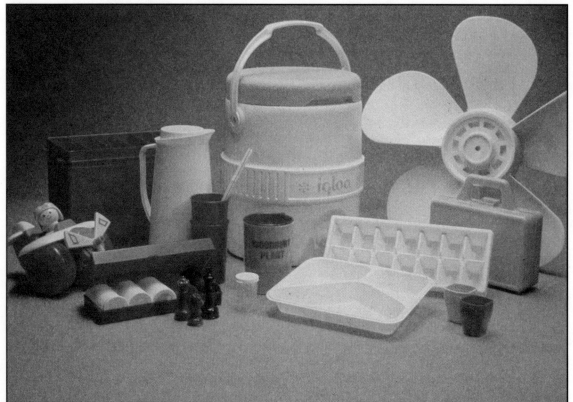

Monument Valley is part of the Colorado Plateau in western North America. Wind and water have carved the rock into many mesas and buttes.

plateau

A plateau (plah-TOE) is a large, flat area of land that is higher than the land around it. Some plateaus—such as the Colorado Plateau in the American Southwest—cover thousands of square miles.

Plateaus are mostly flat, but in some places they are tilted slightly or have mountains rising from them. Some plateaus have deep canyons cut into them by rivers. One of the deepest and widest of these canyons is the Grand Canyon, cut through the Colorado Plateau by the Colorado River. (*See* **Grand Canyon.**)

A plateau is built of rocks that are laid down in flat layers. The rocks may be sedimentary rocks, such as sandstone or shale, or they may be volcanic rocks, such as basalt. After they are laid down, these flat layers may become slightly tilted in places—as in the area around the Grand Canyon.

In dry places, such as Utah and Arizona, occasional rains can fill streams with water. Erosion by the running water cuts the rocks of a plateau into different shapes. One shape is called a *butte.* A butte is a tall, flat-topped hill. Many buttes are found in Monument Valley, an area in southeastern Utah and northeastern Arizona. There, erosion has carved buttes of many shapes into the bright red sandstone of the Colorado Plateau.

A *mesa* is another shape that erosion can carve in the rocks of a plateau. Like a butte, a mesa is a flat-topped hill, but it covers a much larger area. You could quickly walk all over the top of a butte, but it might take a day or more to walk across a mesa.

Some plateaus were raised up by forces in the earth's *crust*—its outer layer. The same kind of forces build mountains. Other plateaus are built by eruptions from volcanoes. In some parts of the world—such as the Columbia Plateau in the northwestern United States—lava poured out of cracks in the earth, layer after layer, for thousands of years. These layers piled up, one on top of another, until the pile—the plateau—was thousands of feet high.

See also **erosion** and **mountain.**

platinum

The element platinum is a metal with a very high melting point—1772° C (3,222° F). It is often used as a *catalyst*—a substance that starts or speeds up chemical reactions, yet remains unchanged itself.

Since 1974, most new cars sold in the United States have had a *catalytic converter.* This device contains platinum and reduces the air pollutants in an automobile's exhaust. As the harmful gases pass through the catalytic converter, platinum changes them into safer ones.

Platinum is used as a catalyst to make acids, vitamins, medicines, and gasoline. It is also a catalyst in fuel cells—devices that produce electric power. Fuel cells are often used in spacecraft, missiles, and fighter planes.

Platinum is prized for making jewelry. It is easy to shape, and can be stretched into thin wires or spread in broad sheets.

Platinum is scarcer and more costly than gold. About 90,000 kilograms (200,000 pounds) of platinum are produced each year—compared to over 1.6 million kilograms (3½ million pounds) of gold. The Soviet Union and South Africa supply most of the world's platinum. The United States uses one-third of all platinum sold.

platypus

The platypus is a mammal that lives in Australia. Like all mammals, it has hair, and the females have milk glands for nursing their young. The platypus is often called a *duck-bill* because its leathery snout looks like a duck's bill. It also has a broad tail like a beaver's. Including its tail, the adult platypus may be 41 to 55 centimeters (16 to 22 inches) long.

Platypuses spend most of their time in rivers and streams, hunting along the bottom for shrimps, insect larvae, worms, and other food. Platypuses do not have teeth. They crush and grind their food between hard ridges on their bills.

Platypuses are excellent swimmers. They use their webbed feet and flat tails to move through the water. A platypus can stay underwater for five minutes before coming up to breathe.

The platypus is one of only three mammals that lays eggs. (The other two are echidnas.) The eggs have leathery shells, like reptile eggs. The female prepares an underground nest in which to lay her eggs. The babies are born blind and without any hair. After about four months, they begin to go outside the nest. They stay close to their mother until they are about one year old.

The platypus spends most of its time in or near rivers and streams.

play

A play is a story told by actors. The story and characters are often made up. Some plays are about real people and real events. The actors dress in costumes, wear makeup, and usually perform on a stage in a theater. Plays are a lot of fun to put on and to perform in. Watching a play can show you how different people live, or even help you understand your own life better. Movies and television dramas are also forms of plays.

Some of the earliest plays we know about were written by the ancient Greeks more than 2,500 years ago. Plays have changed very little over the years.

A play is usually written by a person called a *playwright.* He or she writes a *script.* The script includes the actors' words. It may also tell where and when the action takes place. There may be a description of the stage and scenery. There may also be directions for the actors about where to move on stage, what feelings to show, and other details.

Stage Plays In a theater, the stage is usually a raised platform. In today's theaters, it is often at one end of the auditorium. This kind of stage is a little like a picture with a frame around it. A curtain blocks the audience's view until the play begins. Then the curtain opens, and the audience can look into the "picture." Actors enter and leave from the sides and back of the stage.

Sometimes, the stage is in the center of the auditorium, and the audience sits around it. The actors come and go either by walking through the audience or by passing through trapdoors in the floor of the stage.

In England in the 1600s, a stage was very complicated—it had six parts. On the main level, a large stage jutted out into the audience. A smaller inner stage was at the back. On an upper level, there was an upper stage and three balconies. Actors could step out onto the balconies to speak their lines.

A stage play is usually divided into parts, called *acts.* A very short play has only one act, without any interruption. Longer plays have several acts and usually at least one *intermission*—a short rest period for actors and audience. An act may be divided into smaller parts, called *scenes.*

In addition to the actors, it takes many skilled and talented people to plan and put on a play. The director is in charge of how the play will be performed. He or she works with a team of people—a lighting designer, set designer, costume director, makeup director, and stage manager. Each of these people has several helpers. The director also guides the actors in how to act their parts. The prop manager plans and gathers the *props*—all the furniture and other objects needed by the actors on stage. Prop managers know where to find almost anything. By working together, the actors, the director, and the people in charge of makeup, costumes, lighting, props, and scenery bring a play alive.

Amateurs (left) perform in a high school musical. Husband and wife Hume Cronyn and Jessica Tandy (right) were professional actors for more than 40 years.

Backstage in a theater, there is much work to be done. Sets and props hang along the wall as a worker paints posters to advertise a new production.

Kinds of Plays   The ancient Greeks wrote and performed two kinds of plays—tragedy and comedy. A *tragedy* is a serious play and nearly always has an unhappy ending. A *comedy* usually makes the audience laugh and nearly always has a happy ending. (*See* **comedy** and **tragedy**.)

Greek plays used music and dance as well as spoken words. Today, no one is sure what this music or dancing was like. But we have the scripts for some Greek plays and still perform them just using the words. One of the "characters" in Greek plays is the *chorus* —a group of people who comment on what is happening.

People of other countries wrote different kinds of plays. During the Middle Ages in Europe, people performed religious dramas about saints and characters from the Bible. In Italy, people wrote short comedies that were partly made up by the actors as they went along.

The greatest playwright in the English language was William Shakespeare. He wrote for playhouses in London in the late 1500s and early 1600s. Shakespeare wrote great tragedies such as *Hamlet* and *Romeo and Juliet*. He also wrote many comedies and *tragicomedies*—plays that were part tragedy and part comedy. (*See* **Shakespeare, William**.)

In Italy around the time of Shakespeare, people began writing plays in which the characters sang instead of spoke. These musical plays came to be known as *operas*. Later, the French planned stage productions that used dancers. These shows grew into *ballet*. (*See* **opera** and **ballet**.)

Early settlers in America believed that stage shows were sinful. For many years, there were hardly any theaters. In the late 1700s, many theaters were built in the eastern cities. Actors put on plays of Shakespeare and other English playwrights. They

Costumes and special effects help create an eerie scene. Costumes turn the actors into ugly witches, and lights shine on "smoke" rising from the giant cauldron.

also produced popular plays by Americans.

In the 1800s, the *melodrama* was a popular kind of play. In a melodrama, the audience knows right away who are the good and bad characters. People cheered for the hero and heroine, and they booed and hissed the villains. (*See* **melodrama.**)

In the 1900s, a new kind of stage play called the *American musical* grew up in the theaters of New York. The characters spoke most of their lines, but sometimes they sang and danced. People across the country soon learned the songs from these musicals. Before long, many musicals were made into movies. *The Sound of Music* and *West Side Story* are two popular movie musicals.

After 1900, there were many new ways for people to enjoy plays. The movies made it possible for people in very small towns to see great actors. But for many years, the movies were silent. About the same time, radio stations began broadcasting radio plays. People could hear radio actors, but could not see them. Later, movies had sound, and television made it possible for people to see and hear plays at home. (*See* **movie.**)

Today, most cities have theaters where plays are performed. In New York City, many of the large, old theaters are near Broadway. Washington, D.C., Los Angeles, Minneapolis, and Chicago are other cities known for their theaters.

See also **actors and acting.**

SOME DRAMATISTS AND PLAYS OF THE 1900s
Name (Country), *Play*

Anton Chekhov (Russia), *The Cherry Orchard*
August Strindberg (Sweden), *A Dream Play*
George Bernard Shaw (Ireland/England), *St. Joan*
Sean O'Casey (Ireland), *Juno and the Paycock*
Samuel Becket (Ireland), *Waiting for Godot*
Eugene O'Neill (U.S.), *The Iceman Cometh*
Tennessee Williams (U.S.), *The Glass Menagerie*

Pluto

Pluto is the ninth planet from the sun in our solar system. We think it is the planet farthest from the sun. On average, Pluto's orbit is 5.9 billion kilometers (3⅔ billion miles) away from the sun. Earth's orbit is 150 million kilometers (93 million miles) away.

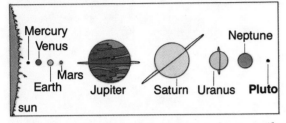

All the planets orbit the sun in a path shaped like a flattened circle. Of all the planets, Pluto has the flattest orbit. In fact, Pluto's orbit is sometimes inside the orbit of its neighbor, Neptune. So for part of its journey—about one-tenth of it—Pluto is closer to the sun than is Neptune. It takes almost 250 Earth years for Pluto to orbit the sun.

Pluto is so far away that we do not know very much about it for certain. We know that Pluto is not made of solid rock, the way Earth is. Instead, scientists think it may be a ball of frozen gases. It is certainly very cold there. Scientists think temperatures reach about −220° C (−360° F) at the planet.

Pluto is about the same size as Earth's moon. It is so small and its orbit is so unusual that some scientists think it is not a planet at all. It may be a moon that has escaped Neptune's orbit. Yet Pluto has a moon of its own, called Charon.

See also **solar system.**

plutonium

Plutonium is a radioactive element and a metal. It is used in nuclear weapons and to power spacecraft. It is so radioactive and poisonous that even the smallest amount of plutonium can cause cancer and death. (*See* **radioactivity.**)

Only a tiny amount of plutonium is found in nature. Most is made in nuclear power plants. The fuel rods in a nuclear reactor are made of uranium. As the uranium produces the heat used to make electric power, it also produces a small amount of plutonium. When the uranium fuel is used up, the plutonium can be separated from the fuel wastes. (*See* **nuclear power.**)

Plutonium was first made in 1940. By 1945, there was enough plutonium to make one of the first atomic bombs. In a bomb that uses plutonium, pieces of plutonium are kept apart from each other until the bomb is set off. When they are quickly brought together, the bomb explodes with tremendous force. (*See* **nuclear weapon.**)

People who handle plutonium have to be very careful to store it so there is never too much of it in one place.

Plymouth

Plymouth was the settlement founded in 1620 by the Pilgrims. Seeking religious freedom, they sailed from England on a ship called the *Mayflower*. They landed on the Massachusetts coast, about 40 miles (64 kilometers) south of the present-day city of Boston.

The place they chose for their colony had once been an Indian village. It had a stream and land cleared of trees. It also had a hill, where they could build a fort.

By 1640, the colony included newer settlements to the north and east of the first settlement. The colony's *freemen*—adult males who were heads of families—met once a year to discuss the colony's problems, make laws, and establish taxes.

Until 1628, fur trading was the colony's main source of income. Then people settled the Massachusetts Bay Colony. The Pilgrims prospered by selling them corn and cattle.

Eventually, the Massachusetts Bay Colony grew larger and more important than Plymouth. It had a better harbor—Boston—and it was better able to defend itself against attacks by Indians, the Dutch, and the French. (*See* **Indian Wars.**)

The Plimoth Plantation is a re-creation of the original Plymouth Colony. People work and dress there the way the Pilgrims did in the 1620s.

In 1691, the Plymouth Colony became part of the Massachusetts Bay Colony. The town of Plymouth is still in Massachusetts. If you go there, you can tour Plimoth Plantation, which has been built to look like the original settlement.

See also **Mayflower** and **Pilgrims.**

poetry

Poetry uses language in a special way. The words in poetry are carefully chosen to build a flowing rhythm and to bring pictures to mind. The blend of sounds, pictures, and rhythms creates moods, such as joy, sadness, excitement, worry, fear, or courage.

A poem's rhythm helps to set the mood. In some poems, the rhythm races. In others, it gently rolls. You may have learned poems by clapping your hands to their rhythm.

The sounds in words are important to poetry's rhythm. One example is this line from a poem by Emily Dickinson: "I like to see it lap the miles." *Like, lap,* and *miles* repeat the consonant *l. Like* and *miles* repeat the vowel sound *i.*

Rhyming words—words whose final syllables sound alike—also add to the rhythm. In some poems, the last word in every line rhymes. More often, only some of the lines end in rhymes, and many times, none of the lines end in rhymes. (*See* **rhyme.**)

A poet may create word pictures by comparing one thing to another. One way to do this is by using a *simile*—a comparison that uses the words "like" or "as." When A. A. Milne wrote "Jonathon Jo has a mouth like

---

A poem that leaves a picture in your mind:

> so much depends
> upon
>
> a red wheel
> barrow
>
> glazed with rain
> water
>
> beside the white
> chickens.

— William Carlos Williams

A verse from a poem that uses strong rhythm and sounds:

The wind was a torrent of darkness among the gusty trees,
The moon was a ghostly galleon tossed upon cloudy seas,
The road was a ribbon of moonlight over the purple moor,
And the highwayman came riding —
    Riding — riding —
The highwayman came riding, up to the old inn-door.

— Alfred Noyes

an 'O,' " he was using a simile. You see the round shape of Jonathon Jo's mouth.

A *metaphor,* too, creates a word picture. It compares two things, but does not use *like* or *as.* Dinah Mulock Craik used a metaphor when she wrote about a dandelion—"With my shield of yellow, and my blade of green." She compares the flower and its leaf to a soldier with a shield and sword. The metaphor also compares the small size and weakness of a flower with a soldier prepared to fight.

If you recite a poem, you can hear the flow of the sounds and the rhythm. The poem may even sound like music. Poetry with a strong musical quality is called *lyrical.* Lyrical poems are short and express feelings.

There are several kinds of lyrical poems. Some, such as haiku and limericks, have a set length. Haiku, a Japanese form, has three lines. The first line has five syllables, the second has seven, and the third has five. A limerick has five lines. The first, second, and last lines end in the same rhyming sound. The third and fourth lines end with another rhyming sound. (*See* **limerick.**)

A nonsense poem:

The panther is like a leopard,
Except it hasn't been peppered.
Should you behold a panther crouch,
Prepare to say Ouch.
Better yet, if called by a panther,
Don't anther.

— Ogden Nash

Some poetry—called *narrative poetry*—tells a story. *Paul Revere's Ride* and *Hiawatha,* by Henry Wadsworth Longfellow, are narrative poems. Short narrative poems called *ballads* are often sung. Very long narrative poems are called *epics.* They tell stories about heroes from history and myths. Homer's *Iliad* and *Odyssey,* for example, are about the adventures of Greek heroes. (*See* **Homer** and **myths and legends.**)

Some plays are written as poetry. This is called *dramatic poetry.* The plays of William Shakespeare are examples of dramatic poetry. (*See* **Shakespeare, William.**)

Poetry is very old. People were reciting or singing poems long before they learned how to write. All human societies have poetry. It may have begun as the chanting of magic spells. Early poetry that has survived often has to do with magic and religion. Sacred texts of many religions were at first recited as poetry. Parts of the Bible and of Hinduism's Vedas are in verse. Before they were written, people kept the words alive in their memories. Each new generation memorized the verses. Poetry was used partly because people wanted a special way to express their religious feelings. Poetry is also easier to memorize than *prose*—ordinary language.

Today, you can read poems in magazines and books, or hear them read aloud. There are recordings of poems, and many poets read their poems in public.

See also **Hughes, Langston; Carroll, Lewis; Mother Goose; and Stevenson, Robert Louis.**

84

poison

Any substance that can harm or kill you is a poison. Poisons can enter the body if you eat, drink, or breathe them. Poisons can also be absorbed through the skin. Some of the most common poisons include cleansers, detergents, insect sprays, rat poisons, lighter fluid, gasoline, and even some plants. Many glues and paints are poisonous. Pills may look like candy, but they may be poisonous. Spoiled food and medicines may be poisons, too. Most cases of poisoning occur around the house or on farms.

Poisons harm the body in different ways. Drain cleaner will burn and eat away any part of the body it touches. Carbon monoxide gas gets into the bloodstream and prevents the body from getting enough oxygen. Weed killers, insecticides, and rat poisons may destroy nerves, paralyze muscles, or make the inside of the body bleed.

The containers of some poisons are marked with a skull and crossbones. This is a danger sign that should always be heeded. Some containers have labels that tell you what to do if the poison has been swallowed. But many poisons, such as bleaches, detergents, and fingernail polish remover, have no warning labels.

To avoid poisoning, never touch anything or put it in your mouth if you do not know what it is. When you are out playing, do not taste berries or mushrooms—many are very poisonous. Do not breathe in fumes and sprays. Keep poisons where animals and small children cannot get to them.

Signs of poisoning include vomiting, stomachache, burns around the mouth, sweating, strange breathing, spasms, and passing out. If you think someone has been poisoned, tell an adult at once. The grown-up can give the victim first aid, or, if you are calling on the telephone, tell you what to do. Then call a doctor, hospital, or poison-control center. Keep their telephone numbers posted near your telephone. Many communities have a telephone number to dial in emergencies. This number is usually "911." You can also dial "O" to reach the telephone operator.

If the poison was swallowed and the person is awake, have the person drink a lot of milk or water, to dilute the poison.

Try to identify the poison. Save the container. If the victim has vomited, save some of the vomit. This will help the doctor know how to treat the victim. Proper first aid and treatment depend on knowing what caused the poisoning.

See also **first aid** and **plant poisons.**

The skull and crossbones (bottom left) means "poison." A few mushrooms and green plants and many household products contain dangerous poisons.

Poland

Capital: Warsaw
Area: 120,725 square miles (312,678 square kilometers)
Population (1985): about 37,233,000
Language: Polish

Poland is the second-largest nation in central Europe. Only the Soviet Union is larger. Poland is about the size of the state of New Mexico, but has many more people. It faces the Baltic Sea on the north and shares borders with the Soviet Union, Czechoslovakia, and East Germany.

Poland's Baltic coast is low and flat. The port city of Gdańsk is on the Baltic Sea. Moving inland, the land is hilly and dotted with many lakes. A low plain covers the central region—Poland's chief agricultural area. Farmers grow barley, potatoes, rye, and wheat. Poland's capital and largest city, Warsaw, is here.

A region of low hills farther south contains one of the world's largest deposits of coal. Coal is the fuel used to run the factories in the area. Poland has modern factories that

A square in Warsaw, the Polish capital.

produce heavy machinery, ships, iron, steel, and textiles.

Along the southern border with Czechoslovakia, the land becomes very mountainous. The Sudetic Mountains are covered with forests. The rocky Carpathian Mountains rise to more than 8,000 feet (2,400 meters) above sea level.

Slavic peoples have lived in the region for 4,000 years. During the 1300s, they united to form an empire. The empire remained strong for about 200 years.

Then Poland began to lose territory to nearby nations. Invaders from Sweden and the Ukraine (now part of the Soviet Union) seized much of Poland's land in the 1600s. In the 1700s, Austria, Russia, and the German state of Prussia divided Poland.

Polish people fought throughout the 1800s to regain control of their land. In 1918, Poland became an independent nation again. But in 1939, Germany and the Soviet Union each took over a part of Poland. The next year, Germany seized the entire country, and Poland suffered greatly during World War II. (*See* **World War II.**)

After the war ended in 1945, Poland was again a nation, but the Soviet Union controlled the government. Poland now has a communist government and maintains close ties with the Soviet Union.

Before World War II, most Poles lived on farms. Today, about half live in cities. The Communist party frowns on religion, but has not been able to break the people's strong ties to the Roman Catholic Church.

police

Police are government officers who enforce the law, maintain public order, and protect the community.

Every country in the world has a police system. In the United States, there are around 40,000 separate police forces. They are run by city, county, and state governments. There are also police agencies run by the federal government.

Police officers in U.S. cities and towns perform a wide variety of jobs. Their main tasks are patrol duty, traffic control, and investigation of crime. They also keep order among large crowds at parades and demonstrations. They look for people who are lost and try to rescue those in danger.

Large police forces often have specialized units. For example, a *bomb squad* investigates bomb threats. A *hostage team* handles cases in which criminals hold people captive. Most members of such units work at other assignments until their special skills are required.

Patrol duty is an important function of the local police force. Patrol officers walk or drive back and forth through their *beat*—an area assigned to them. They look mainly for any signs of crime, but they are also alert for other trouble, such as fires or accidents. Police on patrol keep in touch with headquarters by two-way radio. Headquarters may send them to investigate a reported crime or other emergency.

Police officers stay in touch with each other and with headquarters by radio.

Traffic police promote safety on public streets and highways. They direct traffic and enforce laws against speeding, illegal parking, and other traffic violations. If there is an accident, they find out what happened and help anyone who is injured.

Special police officers, called *detectives,* investigate crimes. They look for clues and interview *witnesses*—people who saw the crime. They find and talk to *suspects*—people who may have committed the crime. Because detectives do not wear uniforms, they are sometimes called *plainclothes officers.* (*See* **crime.**)

Various police experts help detectives to conduct an investigation. A *police photographer* takes pictures of the crime scene. A *ballistics expert* tests any bullets to find out which gun fired them. Other experts examine fingerprints, bloodstains, tire tracks, samples of hair and cloth, and other clues. If people saw the crime, a *police artist* may use their descriptions to draw a picture of the criminal.

Some police officers are assigned to carry out secret investigations. These officers, known as *undercover agents,* gather information about criminal activities such as gambling and drug dealing.

A police artist uses a computer to help make a sketch of a wanted person.

Police departments keep detailed records for use in future investigations. These records include fingerprints, photographs, crime reports, and lists of all arrests. Local police departments may also consult the huge files kept by the FBI—the Federal Bureau of Investigation.

Every state except Hawaii has some kind of state police force. (Hawaii has county police.) The duties of state police vary from state to state, but their main task is to enforce state highway laws. State police are often called *troopers.*

The most famous law-enforcement agency of the federal government is the FBI. It deals with crimes that violate United States laws. There are a number of other federal police. Some patrol the borders of the United States to keep immigrants from entering the country illegally. Others work to stop shipments of illegal drugs. The Secret Service is a special police force that guards the president and other government officials. Secret Service police also enforce the laws against *counterfeit*—imitation—money. (*See* **Federal Bureau of Investigation.**)

polio

Polio—short for *poliomyelitis*—is a disease that attacks the brain and spinal cord. It most often affects children between 4 and 15 years old, but it can also affect adults. Polio is caused by a virus.

Infection by a polio virus does not always cause severe illness. Some people have symptoms, such as fever and vomiting, that disappear after 24 hours. More serious cases start with these same symptoms, but the symptoms do not go away. Instead, other symptoms develop. The back and neck become stiff and painful. The muscles become weak, and movement becomes difficult.

No medicine has yet been found that cures polio. The most important treatment is complete bed rest. As the patient begins to recover, his or her limbs should be moved gently to strengthen the muscles.

After the disease passes, most polio victims can lead their lives as they did before. Some may need to use braces or crutches. Only a few are permanently paralyzed.

Polio was a common disease in the 1940s and early 1950s. Jonas Salk developed the first polio vaccine in 1955. In 1961, Albert Sabin developed a polio vaccine that could be taken by mouth. Today, there are very few cases of polio in the United States, thanks to these vaccines.

See also **Salk, Jonas** and **vaccine.**

political party

A political party is an organization of people who have certain political beliefs in common. The party works to elect its own people to public office. If elected, these people—the party's *candidates*—are supposed to carry out the party's goals.

Some countries permit only one party. This party controls the government, and everyone has to vote for its candidates. In the Soviet Union, for example, the Communist party is the only party allowed.

In countries with a democratic form of government, people are free to form and to join political parties. Some democratic countries, such as France and Italy, have many parties. The United States today has two main political parties.

The Constitution of the United States does not mention political parties. George Washington, the first president, did not belong to a party. The first parties began to form as soon as Washington's term started. (*See* **Washington, George.**)

Soon, the political parties were holding meetings called *conventions* to *nominate* —choose—candidates to run for office. At their convention, each party decided on its *platform*—its political goals. Political parties got involved in all levels of government—city, state, and national.

In the United States, the two main political parties are the Democratic party and the Republican party. Sometimes, a third party has

In the United States, the Democratic Party uses the donkey as a symbol. The Republican Party uses the elephant.

been important in U.S. politics. A third party may form by breaking away from one of the main parties. Or a third party may be started to support a particular cause. For example, the Populist Party of the 1890s was formed to help farmers and workers.

The Democratic party began in the late 1700s as the Democratic-Republican party. In 1824, it broke into several groups, including the Democratic party. Thomas Jefferson and Andrew Jackson were two of the early Democratic presidents. (*See* **Jefferson, Thomas** and **Jackson, Andrew.**)

The Republican party was formed in 1854. Abraham Lincoln was the first Republican president. He was elected in 1860. (*See* **Lincoln, Abraham.**)

In the late 1800s and early 1900s, the Republican party tended to be the stronger party. It elected more presidents and often had more members in Congress than did the Democratic party. The Democrats were very strong in the 1930s and early 1940s. During that period, Americans elected Franklin D. Roosevelt, a Democrat, president four times. (*See* **Roosevelt, Franklin.**)

Since the middle 1940s, the two parties have had about equal power. Republican presidents have spent more years in the White House, but there have been more Democrats elected to Congress.

Polk, James K., *see* presidents of the U.S.

pollination

In flowering plants, pollination is the process of moving pollen from the male part of a flower to the female part of the same kind of flower. In cone-bearing plants, it is moving pollen from a male cone to a female cone of the same kind. After pollination takes place, seeds begin to form.

Flowering plants that have flowers containing both the female and male parts sometimes pollinate themselves. This is called *self-pollination.* When pollen from one flower is moved to another flower, it is called *cross-pollination.*

Pollination happens in various ways. One of the simplest kinds of pollination is by the wind. Cone-bearing trees, grasses, and many trees with small flowers are pollinated this way. You may have seen small clouds of yellow "dust" blown from trees. This is pollen being carried by the wind. The allergies that many people have in the spring are caused by pollen in the air. Since much of the pollen that causes the allergies is from grasses, the allergy is called *hay fever.*

At top, a bumblebee picks up pollen from one flower. At bottom, the pollen brushes off the bee and pollinates another flower.

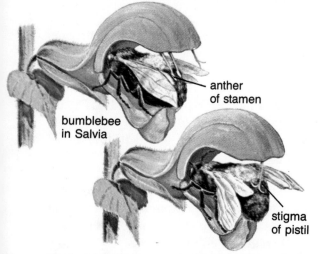

bumblebee
in Salvia

anther
of stamen

stigma
of pistil

Most other flowers are usually pollinated by insects, birds, or other animals. You have probably seen bees or butterflies flying from flower to flower. While they are taking food from a flower, pollen sticks to their bodies. When they visit the next flower, some of the pollen rubs off. Most *pollinators*—the insect or animal that carries pollen—prefer certain kinds of flowers, so the chances of their pollinating the right flowers as they feed are very good.

Often, the shape of the pollinator matches the shape of the flower. So the pollinator is sure to pick up pollen and leave some behind when it feeds. Hummingbirds usually pollinate bright red or orange tube-shaped flowers. A hummingbird's long beak fits into the flower's deep throat.

Brightly-colored flowers are usually pollinated by animals that are active during the day. White and light-colored flowers are usually pollinated by animals active at night. The most common night pollinators are moths and bats.

Pollen is made up of tiny grains. These grains can be seen clearly only under a microscope. When *magnified*—made to appear larger—pollen grains have patterns of ridges, pits, and little spines. Each kind of pollen has its own pattern. Scientists who study pollen can tell what plant the pollen came from just by looking at the pattern.

See also plant breeding.

Pollock, Jackson

Jackson Pollock was an American painter. He is known for his paintings made by dripping paint onto the canvas.

Pollock was born in Wyoming in 1912. He began making sculpture when he was 13. At age 17, he started studying painting at the Art Students League in New York City.

During the 1930s, Pollock created realistic paintings. From 1938 to 1942, he worked for the Federal Arts Project, a government program that paid artists to decorate public buildings.

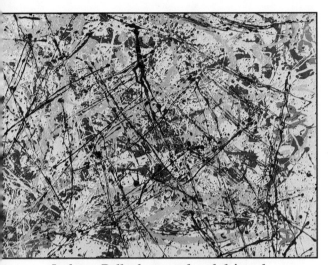

Jackson Pollock poured and dripped paints to create his paintings.

Pollock became well known during the 1940s. In 1947, he changed his painting method. Instead of standing the canvas on an easel, he laid it on the floor or fastened it to a wall. Then he poured and dripped the paint directly onto the canvas. He moved it around with sticks, trowels, or knives. Sometimes he mixed in sand or broken glass. His style of painting was called *abstract expressionism*. It showed lines and movement rather than recognizable things. It also expressed feelings or moods.

When Jackson Pollock died, in 1956, many people still thought abstract expressionism was not really art. But they soon began to realize that Pollock's new way of painting was exciting and interesting.

---

pollution, *see* **air pollution; water pollution**

Polo, Marco

Marco Polo was one of the most famous travelers in history. At a time when few people ever left their hometowns, he journeyed from Italy all the way to China—then known as Cathay. He wrote a book about his travels. In it, Europeans read about lands and customs they had not imagined existed.

Marco was born in Venice, Italy, around the year 1254. His father and an uncle soon left on a trading trip. While they were away, Marco's mother died. He was raised by an aunt and uncle, and he was educated to be a merchant.

Marco's father and uncle traveled to Russia and China. In China, they met Kublai Khan, the Mongol emperor who ruled there. When they left China, Kublai Khan invited them to return with learned men who could tell him about Christianity.

Marco's father and uncle began their second trip to China in 1271, taking 17-year-old Marco with them. First they sailed across the Mediterranean Sea to western Asia. Two missionaries began the trip with them, but turned back. The Polos traveled by camel across Asia to China. After about three and a half years, they reached Kublai Khan's summer palace at Shang-tu. Kublai Khan gave them a warm welcome.

Marco Polo learned languages easily and had a good memory, so Kublai Khan sent him on several special missions. He went to southern and northern China, India, and possibly Burma. After his journeys, he reported back to Kublai Khan.

The Polos stayed in China more than 15 years. Then the emperor asked them to take a Mongol princess to Persia, where she was to be married. In 1290, they started their trip by sea. On the way, they stopped at lands now called Vietnam, Malaysia, and Sumatra, and the island of Sri Lanka.

The Polos said good-bye to the Mongol princess at Hormuz, near the Gulf of Oman. They then traveled overland to Venice, arriving in 1295. They had been away for 24 years and traveled nearly 15,000 miles (24,000 kilometers)!

Many Venetians thought the Polos had died. They did not recognize the travelers, and did not believe their amazing stories. So the men dressed in Chinese silks and held a big banquet. Then they slit open their clothes to reveal the precious jewels they had carried back.

At the time of the Polos' return, Venice was at war with Genoa, another Italian city. In 1296, Marco was captured by the Genoese. He spent the next two years in prison. While in prison, he decided to write a book about his travels. He included descriptions of lands he had not visited but had heard about from other travelers. Another prisoner wrote down Polo's story.

Polo's book, called *Description of the World,* was very popular. It was written before the invention of the printing press, so copies were made by hand. The first printed copy was made in 1477.

Description of the World was the first European book to tell of China's riches and huge size. Polo was the first European to report on many parts of the East, including Burma, Laos, Thailand, Japan, and India. He described China's Gobi Desert and the "white bears" (polar bears) of Siberia.

Polo described some fantastic things that later became well known in Europe. For example, in China he saw "stones that burned." These burning stones were pieces of coal. He also saw the Chinese using paper money. Not until much later did Europeans use paper money instead of heavy coins.

Polo's book made Europeans curious about Asia and other lands. Christopher Columbus was one of the many explorers who studied it. When he sailed from Spain in 1492, he was looking for the empire of Kublai Khan. Instead, he found the New World of America. (*See* **Columbus, Christopher.**)

Pompeii

Pompeii (pom-PAY) was an ancient Roman city in southern Italy. It was buried about 1,900 years ago when a volcano named Mount Vesuvius erupted. For hundreds of years, the houses and streets lay hidden under tons of ash, stone, and cinders. Then, in the middle 1700s, a farmer struck a wall while digging in his garden. His discovery began years of work to uncover the buried city. The ruins tell us a great deal about daily life in the Roman Empire.

Pompeii was a port near the present-day city of Naples. It stood less than 1 mile (1.6 kilometers) away from Mount Vesuvius. The

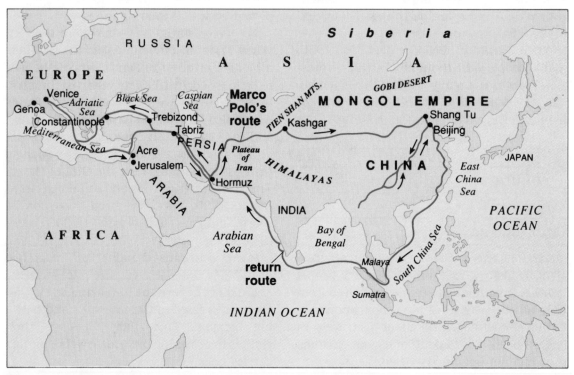

These ruins in Pompeii were buried by volcanic ash from the year 79 until modern times. They help us understand how the ancient Romans lived.

town was built in an oval shape and surrounded by a wall. Its streets crossed each other at right angles. Raised sidewalks lined both sides of the streets. The wheels of wagons and chariots had worn ruts in the streets' paving stones.

The town had many beautiful public buildings. In the center was a *forum*—a square—decorated with statues. Nearby were two theaters, many temples to gods and goddesses, and several public baths.

The houses of traders and craftspeople often had shops facing the street so the owner could do business with people passing by. The houses of wealthy people were built around courtyards that were open to the sky. Colorful paintings decorated the walls. In the floors were *mosaics*—designs made of small pieces of colored stone. One mosaic, showing a chained animal, has the Latin warning *Cave canem*—"Beware of the dog."

Life at Pompeii came to a sudden end on the morning of August 24, A.D. 79. We know a lot about the disaster because Pliny the Younger, a Roman writer, was there and wrote about the event.

Most of the 20,000 people who lived in Pompeii managed to flee. About 2,000 people died from the poisonous fumes and fire. The volcanic ash hardened over the bodies, preserving their forms. Many other things were preserved that tell us how the people of Pompeii lived. A blacksmith's shop was full of objects waiting for repair. Shelves in food stores were lined with loaves of bread and with glass containers of fruits. In a doctor's office, instruments were ready for surgery. An election campaign was going on, and political slogans covered the walls. There were even scribbled messages such as "Marcus loves Livia."

This mosaic showing animals of Egypt was uncovered in Pompeii.

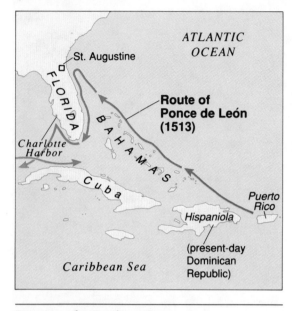

ATLANTIC OCEAN

St. Augustine

FLORIDA

Route of Ponce de León (1513)

B A H A M A S

Charlotte Harbor

C u b a

Puerto Rico

Hispaniola

(present-day Dominican Republic)

Caribbean Sea

Ponce de León, Juan

Juan Ponce de León was a Spanish explorer of North America. He was the first European to visit Florida.

Ponce de León was born in Spain in the late 1400s. He may have sailed to America on the second voyage of Christopher Columbus, in 1493. (*See* **Columbus, Christopher.**)

In the early 1500s, Ponce de León helped defeat the Indians in what is now the Dominican Republic. He then moved to Puerto Rico, defeated the Indians there, and became governor. He was soon wealthy, with gold, slaves, and land. But he wanted more.

The Indians of the Caribbean islands talked about a rich island north of Cuba. Ponce de León was determined to find it. Legend says that he was also looking for a magical spring whose waters would make an old man young again—the Fountain of Youth.

He sailed north in 1513 and landed near the present-day city of St. Augustine. He called the region *Florida*—meaning "full of flowers"—and claimed it for Spain. After exploring the east and west coasts of the Florida peninsula, he sailed back to the Caribbean. Ponce de León did not return to Florida until 1521. He was wounded in an Indian attack and died soon after.

See also **Florida.**

Pony Express

The Pony Express was a special way to send mail from the eastern United States to California. In 1860, when the Pony Express began, California and Oregon were separated from the other states by 1,500 miles of rough and dangerous country. At that time, there were no cars or airplanes, no telephones or telegraphs.

Before the Pony Express, mail to California from the East often took many months to arrive. Some mail was brought by ship down the Atlantic coast and through the Gulf of Mexico to Panama. Then it was carried across Panama and put on a ship that sailed up the Pacific coast. Other mail traveled by train as far as Missouri. Then it was taken by a slow freight wagon across the plains and mountains.

The Pony Express promised that letters would reach California only eight days after they left Missouri. The company had 190 "stations" built along the trail from St. Joseph, Missouri, to Sacramento, California. The stations were about 15 miles apart and provided water, food, and lodging for men and horses.

Pony Express riders changed to a fresh horse every few hours.

Pony Express letters were put in a leather pouch at St. Joseph. A rider took the pouch and galloped out of town, stopping at a station just long enough to change horses. On he rode, for about twelve hours. When he came to the last station on his run, a new rider took the pouch and galloped off.

Many Pony Express riders were still in their teens. They had to weigh less than 130 pounds so that the horses they rode could carry heavy loads of mail. The horses were the fastest and strongest that could be found. The riders had to be strong, too. They rode day and night, and faced storms, Indian attacks, and wild animals. Every pouch of mail except one got through to California.

Less than two years after the Pony Express started, workers finished the first telegraph line connecting the east and west coasts. Suddenly, people could send messages from Boston or New York all the way to California in just a few minutes. There was no longer a need for the Pony Express. But even today we are thrilled by stories of how Pony Express riders braved great danger to achieve their goal.

pope

The pope is the leader of the Roman Catholic Church. He rules the church from Vatican City—a small country in the middle of the city of Rome, Italy.

Roman Catholics believe that Saint Peter was the first pope. They say that Jesus Christ named him head of the church and gave him the "keys to heaven." Two crossed keys are a symbol of the pope. (*See* **Peter.**)

The pope is also the bishop of Rome. He leads religious services in St. Peter's Church in Vatican City. It is the world's largest church. Many people believe St. Peter's bones are buried under its main altar.

The pope selects *cardinals*—church leaders—to help run the church. When the pope dies, the cardinals elect a new pope.

The pope has many duties and powers. He makes laws for running the church. He

Pope John Paul II blesses a crowd. The pope is leader of the Roman Catholic Church.

makes decisions about what Catholics believe as part of their faith, and about *morals* —what is right and what is wrong. The pope can also decide whether a person has led an especially good life and make that person a saint. Catholics believe that what the pope decides regarding faith and morals is always correct, because he is inspired directly by God when he speaks on these matters.

See also **Roman Catholic Church.**

population

A human population is the total number of people living in an area. The area may be a town, state, nation, or the world. A nation learns the size of its population by conducting a *census*—a count of its people. (*See* **census.**)

The population of the world today is about 5 billion. Almost half of the world's people live in five countries—China, India, the Soviet Union, the United States, and Indonesia.

Nations with large populations are not always more crowded than nations with small populations. How crowded a nation is also

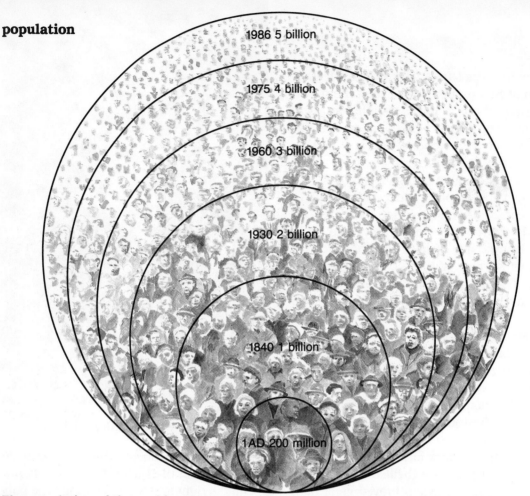

1986 5 billion

1975 4 billion

1960 3 billion

1930 2 billion

1840 1 billion

1 AD 200 million

The population of the world grows very rapidly. For every person on earth in 1830, there are now at least five people.

depends on its size. The number of people living in each square mile (or square kilometer) of an area is called *population density.* One of the most crowded countries in the world is Singapore. Singapore has 10,700 persons per square mile (4,280 per square kilometer).

Some parts of a country may have a greater population density than other parts. For example, few people live in the cold, barren regions of northern Canada. Most Canadians live in the warmer south.

A population usually does not stay the same from year to year. The *birth rate*—the number of births for each 1,000 people—may go up or down. So may the *death rate* —the number of deaths for each 1,000 people. People may move away from an area or move to it. (*See* **immigration.**)

About 10,000 years ago—when humans first settled down and began to grow their own food—the number of people in the world may have been only 5 million. The population grew slowly until around the year 1750. Then the population started to increase quickly. This change was caused by a lower death rate—more people were living longer. Farmers learned how to grow more food on the same amount of land. People also learned to prevent disease by keeping water supplies and medical instruments clean, and by eating a balanced diet.

The world's population reached 1 billion by 1850. Then it doubled—to 2 billion—in less than 100 years. The rapid increase in the number of people in recent times has been called a *population explosion.* Some experts worry that increased population will lead to overcrowding and starvation for millions. Others believe that continued improvements in agriculture will enable farmers to grow enough food for everyone.